How To CUSTOM I
HARLEY-DAVIDSON

Timothy Remus

Motorbooks International
Publishers & Wholesalers ®

First published in 1994 by Motorbooks
International Publishers & Wholesalers, PO Box 2,
729 Prospect Avenue, Osceola, WI 54020 USA

Motorbooks International books are also available
at discounts in bulk quantity for industrial or
sales-promotional use. For details write to Special
Sales Manager at the Publisher's address

Library of Congress Cataloging-in-Publication
Data

Remus, Timothy.
      How to custom paint your Harley–Davidson /
Timothy Remus.
         p.   cm.
      Includes index.
      ISBN 0-87938-861-7
         1. Harley–Davidson motorcycle—Painting.
2. Harley–Davidson motorcycle—Customizing.
I. Title.
      TL448.H3R46   1994
      629.227'5—dc20   93-39572

On the front cover: Radical flames highlight
this Evolution-engined beauty owned and built by
long-time Harley enthusiast Ed Kerr.

Printed and bound in the United States of America

Contents

Acknowledgments

Somehow, each book I write seems to be more work than the one before. I don't know if that means I have written too many, or if I am putting more work into each one as I try to make each better than the last. The books do get easier, however, because each one introduces me to new people whom I can use for references and technical help.

The list of painters, technicians, body men, and paint reps who helped me with this book is a long one. For hands-on help and for letting me into his shop again and again, I have to thank that wild and crazy guy from the east side of St. Paul Minnesota, Mallard Teal. For taking time out of a busy schedule, I have to thank Jon Kosmoski, one of the best-known custom painters anywhere. Lenny Schwartz and Brian Truesdell, two talented pinstripers, let me into their shops as well. I know you guys are good because you make it look so easy.

Greg Smith and Pete Wilson let me tag along as they molded a frame for bike builder Donnie Smith. Thanks, guys. And for technical help, advice, and proofreading, I must thank Jim McGill, paint rep for PPG.

I have to thank my old friend Gordy "Bondo Wizard" Larson for taking one of his free Saturdays to patch up an old Harley tank. Gordy and I have been working on projects together since the days we built forts in the gravel pit near our childhood homes, but that's another story.

I would like to thank just a few more people. Thanks to Doug Thompson, custom car builder without equal, for proofreading the manuscript; Jim Bryntesen of Croix Air for all his help; and Jerry Scherer for answering all my questions.

Of course, I have to thank my lovely and talented wife, Mary, who must think sometimes (though she never says anything) that it would be nice to have a husband with a *regular* job.

Introduction

In writing *How to Custom Paint Your Harley-Davidson,* I tried to be comprehensive. The book starts with a chapter on planning, the most important part of any major project. The following chapters include information about equipping your shop and understanding modern paints. You will also find information on dents, molding frames, and painting engines. The last three chapters describe four paint jobs, step-by-step. (The last of those chapters explains special effects like pinstriping and airbrushing.)

This book is not, however, a customizing manual. For that information, you will need a different book. One suggestion is *How to Customize Your Harley-Davidson,* also available from Motorbooks International.

In writing this book, I have tried to provide enough information and inspiration so the first-time painter would be convinced that he or she could paint a motorcycle. The color paint section is intended again to inspire and excite, to get you out in that garage, working on that motorcycle, making it better than it was. Maybe you will design the bike that will win an award at the next show or one that stands tall when parked outside the local watering hole.

In addition to the basic information, I have presented some advanced techniques. This information will give first-time paint students something to shoot for while it helps more advanced painters move on in a technical as well as creative sense.

I believe we learn best by doing. The next best way to learn is to watch, or read about, someone who performs a certain skill day in and day out. Thus Chapters 7, 8, and 9 take the reader into the shops of Mallard Teal, Jon Kosmoski, and Lenny Schwartz and Brian Truesdell. Between these four men, there are seventy-five years of paint and bodywork experience. As much as possible, I've tried to bring the reader into these pros' shops because there is much to learn from painters of this caliber.

Most of the painting described in this book was done with either PPG or House of Kolor paints. Other good paints and paint systems exist, including BASF and DuPont. I chose to focus on PPG and House of Kolor because 90 percent of the custom building and painting shops that I walked into (whether a car or motorcycle shop) use paints from these manufacturers.

Ultimately, the best way to learn a skill is by practicing it. You hold in your hands a book with much information. But there is no substitute for the school of hard knocks. Go out in the garage and do it. Mix paint into the gun and point that gun at your Harley-Davidson. It is the only way you are really going to learn how to paint.

Chapter 1

Planning

The Most Important Part of Any Big Project

You might think that a planning step is unnecessary. After all, why should you waste your time planning something as simple as a paint job? Wouldn't the time be better spent doing the actual work? There are two reasons for a planning step. First, if you think first and act second, you are more likely to end up with a better paint job. It is too easy to strip the paint and start shooting. The trouble comes later when you realize that, for the same amount of work, you could have had a paint job with more color and better visual impact.

Money is the second reason for thinking first and painting second. Even if you do all your own work, a quality paint job is an expensive undertaking. Urethane paints are expensive, even in small quantities. Lacquer, two-part primers, plastic body filler, and spot filler are not cheap, either. As long as you are going to spend all those bucks, take pains to ensure that the end result is what you originally had in mind. The only way to do that is to carefully plan the whole job.

Where to Start

There are two types of paint jobs: The relatively simple ones that involve only the tank (or tanks) and fenders, and the more extensive jobs that involve both the sheet metal and frame.

The first type is considerably easier. Pulling the tank (or tanks) and fenders off most Harleys is a straightforward job, easily done in one afternoon.

A Cory Harder design done for Drag Specialties (the bike was eventually built by Donnie Smith). Note the flowing lines and futuristic shape. You may not have Cory's tal- *ents, but anyone can make a photocopy of a photograph and pencil in changes or create a new color scheme.*

*Same bike, different paint and graphics. Note how the
new paint brightens the whole bike and how the scallops
give it a sense of motion.*

*Another of Cory's designs. This modern dresser has been
lowered and the bags have been trimmed to reduce bulk.*

*Try to imagine this bike in one solid color—it certainly
would not be the same machine.*

If the bike is an FLH or late-model Ultra with bags, you are in for more work, but the job is still just a matter of unbolting the pieces while the basic bike stays intact.

With the fenders, tanks, and other sheet metal parts removed, roll the chassis over to the opposite side of your shop and start painting the sheet metal. When the paint job is finished, you need only reverse the process. Soon, you have a great-looking motorcycle sitting in your shop.

The downside to the easy paint job is the fact that you are left with a black chassis (usually). This means that no matter how wild the paint job, you have that colorful paint bolted to a black frame. The other problem is that you'll be limited in the colors you can choose for the sheet metal because they must work with the frame's color.

The alternative to this approach is the complete paint job. That is, a paint job that includes both the sheet metal and the frame. When you paint everything, you have more freedom in the color combinations you choose. You also get a better looking job overall, because *everything* has been painted. You can paint the frame to match or

complement the rest of the bike. By painting the chassis, you also have the opportunity to mold all the welds and joints in the frame. Molding adds work to the total job, but it is one of those things that really sets a custom bike apart from the rest. Painting the entire bike also provides the opportunity to paint all or part of the engine, a growing trend.

Deciding whether to paint the whole shebang or just the sheet metal involves your budget for both time and money and a frank assessment of your skills and commitment. Taking a bike all the way down to the frame is not twice as much work as pulling off just the sheet metal, it is more like six or eight times the work. It means disassembling everything until you have the frame, swingarm, sheet metal, and any accessories sitting in a corner. A complete paint job involves more money, too, because there are more parts to paint and you are likely to find more things to repair or replace.

The complete paint job makes sense if you want a true custom Harley or if the bike has covered many miles and needs to be completely gone

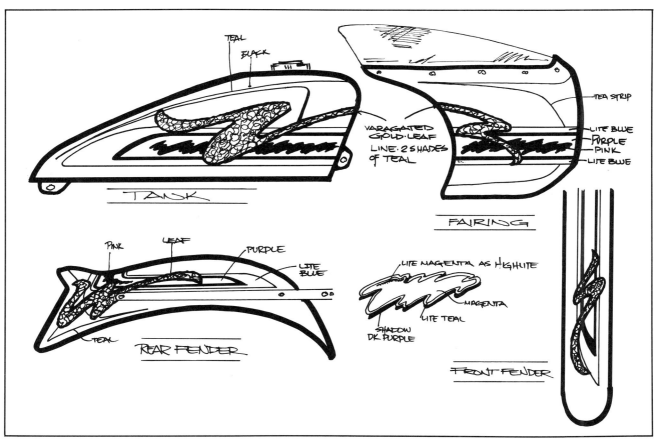

This is the elaborate layout that Lenny Schwartz did before beginning the paint job detailed in Chapter 9. By sketching the paint job before applying any paint, you *can get a pretty good idea what the finished bike will look like and make changes as desired.*

through. If you want to spiff up the old Shovelhead and stay on a tight budget, then just paint the sheet metal and leave the frame in basic black.

A Budget

Grab a sheet of paper and a pencil and figure out a budget for your paint job. If you are just painting the sheet metal, you might be surprised at the high cost of the materials. If you are painting the total machine, consider how much money will be necessary to paint all those parts. Decide now if you are going to go further in hock and send some of the parts to a chrome-plating shop or if you are going to add expensive parts from the Custom Chrome or Drag Specialties catalogs.

Planning a budget forces you to think about the total cost of the job. This is the time to make those hard choices between painting the engine or having the cases polished. Because there is never as much money for a project as you would like, the written budget will help you get the most visual bang for a given amount of hard-earned greenbacks.

Include time as well as money in your budget. Things always take longer than expected, so factor in extra time for each operation. Be sure to leave plenty of time for parts that are farmed out, like chrome plating. This part of the budget process helps get things done on time and avoids those all-night sessions (when the work tends to get sloppy) two days before Sturgis or Daytona.

Choosing a Color

When you choose a color, you choose the look of the bike. A basic black bike with a few chrome accessories is just that—basic black. A bike with a two-tone candy red paint job with different base coats will have a much different look. You can use paint to make a bike look mild or wild, modern or old. A paint job with strong horizontal lines can make a bike look longer and lower, vertical stripes can do the opposite.

Find photos of bikes similar to yours painted in the colors you are considering. Look through magazines, like *American Iron* and others, and cut out pictures of the bikes you like. Take photographs at shows and rallies. Study your pictures and photographs. Which colors have the greatest impact? Which bikes get the most attention? Don't forget to plan the pinstripes, which are usually

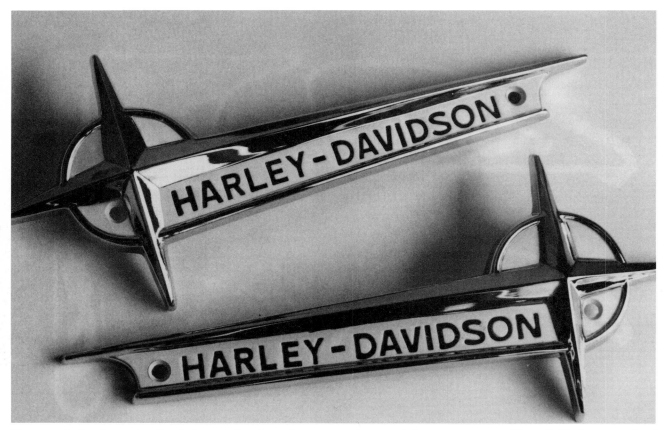

If you are trying to create a "period correct" motorcycle or the illusion that the bike is old, you may want to include older Harley logos as part of your plan. The design seen *here, and dozens more, are still available from your local Harley dealer.*

added at the end of the paint job. Carefully chosen stripes can add the final accent to a great paint job. Like the frosting on a cake, stripes do not seem a big part of the job, but it is hard to imagine a paint job without some striping.

You might start choosing a color for your scooter by looking through the paint chip books available from most paint manufacturers. Another good aid is the Pantone Matching System (PMS) book (see Chapter 9), which printers use to determine the right color for a certain printing job. The PMS book includes hundreds of different colors and lets you hold different colors next to each other to determine their compatibility.

It can be hard to imagine an entire bike painted the color of one little chip sitting among a thousand others. Even tougher is imagining what a bike will look like with a two-tone paint job based on two little chips.

Professional designers and motorcycle builders often create several sketches and drawings before starting a project. In the same way, you can find ways to approximate what your finished bike will look like. After you have studied other bikes, and you think you know what you

want, take some pictures of your own bike, make photocopies of them, enlarge the copies, and hand color them with markers. You probably cannot duplicate the color, but you can see how different color combinations and graphic designs look on the bike.

If you need to see the color on a surface larger than a paint chip, bite the bullet and buy a small can of that color. Spray some on an old panel. Doug Thompson, a professional car painter and builder, uses old light bulbs. He paints a series of bulbs in different colors and carries them into different lighting situations to see how they look. The bulbs' curved shape helps him to see how the highlights will look (especially useful on the curved panels of motorcycles).

If you are building a really killer bike, you might want to hire a designer, like Thom Taylor (better known for car work), Cory Harder, or Eric Aurand, to actually draw your bike in various colors using different graphic designs. Though it involves an added expense, this is a good way to bring fresh ideas into your painting project.

What It All Means

The planning and budgeting stages are exercises designed to make you think about your project. Too many of us paint our bikes and automatically choose the same color as our buddy's bike or one we saw in a magazine. Like a Monday-morning quarterback, it is only after the job is finished that we realize the bike would have looked better in another color or with a slightly different design.

Avoid the "hindsight is always 20-20" blues, and think about the paint job before you pick up the paint gun.

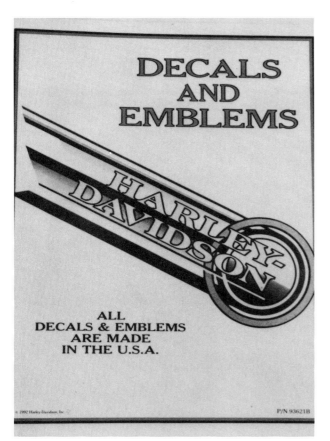

This catalog of the various logo and decal offerings is available at your Harley-Davidson dealer.

Another older logo available for your retro Harley. These glue on so you do not have to weld or drill on your nice tanks.

11

Sly's old FL looks great and benefits from a great Paul Erpenbeck paint job done in Deep Red and Pearl White.

The paint you choose for your bike needs to complement the rest of the machine.

Painted in reds with lavender panels, the colorful paint on Wayne's FXR works well with the bike's radical look.

Chapter 2

Your Shop

What Tools to Buy and Why

You cannot overhaul engines without at least a small shop and some minimum amount of equipment. Paint and body work are no different. Even though some of your friends might have elaborate shops with plenty of light, lots of space and a whole chest of Snap-On tools, the essential equipment for painting is actually rather minimal. In fact, well-known car and bike painter Jon Kosmos-

ki tells stories of painting motorcycle parts in his mother's basement until the fumes got so bad that she threw him out.

Equipping a Basic Shop

For a basic shop, a one stall garage is nice, though you can actually work with less. But no matter the work area's size, it must be well lit with

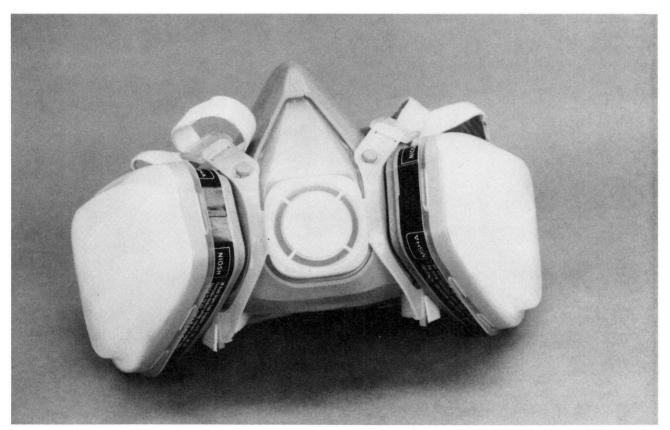

Safety first. Spraying with any non-isocyanate catalyzed paint requires a charcoal filter type respirator like this one. The better respirators have pre-filters to extend the life of the charcoal filters. Store the charcoal filters or the whole mask in a sealed can or plastic bag when not in use to get maximum life from the filters.

good ventilation. You need compressed air (more later), heat (if you live in the Great White North), and many electrical outlets. The shop also needs a floor that can be kept clean; access to running water is a nice bonus.

Remember that while you need ventilation, you also need dust control during those periods when you are spraying paint. An easy way to ventilate a garage is to open the door about one foot and stretch some Dustlok filter material (made by Fiberbond Air Filtration Products) across that opening. At the end of the door, slide in a ventilation fan, to push air out of the shop. Air drawn in will pass through and be filtered by the Dustlok material.

The fan you use to push air out of the shop should be one designed specifically for that job. The fan should run without any sparks at the motor brushes and no chance to ignite the flammable fumes often present in a paint shop. The flammability question affects your heat source choice,

too. If you are lucky enough to live in Southern California, then you may not need heat at all.

If your shop requires heat, put the heat source in another room and duct the heat in. Use a non-flame heat source, like electric baseboards (though there is probably a spark as the thermostat cycles on and off), or shut the heater off when fumes are present. Remember that gas and solvent fumes are usually heavier than air, so they gather near the floor. This means that if there are any flames, pilot lights, or sparks in your shop, you must keep them as high above the floor as possible.

To paint both well and safely, you need to heat the shop to a nice, steady 70 degrees minimum,

Because of environmental concerns and new laws governing the transfer efficiency of paint guns, there is currently a bewildering array of guns on the market. Pictured is Jon Kosmoski's tool cabinet showing most (not all) of his spray guns.

A conventional, high-pressure siphon spray gun from Sharpe. Painters have used guns like this for decades. New laws and environmental concerns, however, are rapidly making them obsolete.

without too much humidity or an open flame. (Thrifty bikers often use wood heat for their garages, though it's probably not a good idea when the building is filled with gasoline and flammable chemicals.) Many paint jobs have been ruined because the paint was applied at 60 degrees, or because the heat was shut off before the paint could cure.

Shop Tools

Because motorcycles are small, you do not need big, fancy grinders and sanders to do your body and paint work. But you will still need an air compressor, the one tool that will drive so many others in your shop. You might want a small air-powered grinder, and a double-action sander is a nice time-saving tool.

The size of the air compressor you choose will depend to some extent on the type of paint gun you use (more on guns later). When it comes to buying air compressors, the old adage "bigger is better" definitely applies. The trouble of course is that air compressors are not cheap. The tendency for some people is to wait until a 2hp model comes on sale at Sears and then proudly drag that shiny, tiny new unit home.

Most paint manufacturers, however, recommend that you use a compressor with at least 3hp, and some think the minimum figure should be 5hp. Custom painter Jon Kosmoski feels that insufficient compressor capacity causes a high percentage of painting troubles in small paint shops.

Both the equipment you buy and the compressor you use to run that equipment carry a CFM (cubic feet per minute) rating. To calculate a compressor's CFM output, use the guide of 4CFM per horsepower (a 3hp compressor would put out about 12CFM). Pay close attention to these ratings when you shop for equipment.

When shopping for a compressor, remember that the harder it works, the hotter it gets. Soon the air coming out of the compressor heats up too, carrying moisture along with it. In the air hose, near the gun, the air cools and the moisture condenses out of the airstream. It only takes one little spit of water to ruin an otherwise perfect paint job. Hot, overworked compressors also pick up more oil from the compressor's crankcase and pass that along with the hot air in the airstream.

If you have not purchased a compressor yet, save your money and buy a large one. If your compressor is not big enough, or you do not yet own

Air and paint mix as they leave the spray gun. Atomization of the paint occurs in two or three stages. The shape of the paint fan is controlled largely by air leaving the horns of the air cap.

15

one, why not rent one for the first paint job? Renting will leave you with more money to spend on the job itself. You don't want to blow your whole budget just equipping the shop.

In Search of the Holy Grail: A Clean Air Supply

So you bite the bullet and buy a big, killer compressor that looks like it belongs in the back room of the Chevy garage, and you figure your air supply troubles are over. Not exactly. You need more than just a high quantity of air, you also need *quality* air—air that is clean and dry.

Specifically, you need to run the air through lines with enough capacity to prevent a drop in pressure. In addition to being big enough, the air lines must be routed to discourage the passing of impurities from the main line to the feeder tubes. You also want to avoid big temperature changes in the air lines (like when long hoses lay on the garage floor) causing any moisture to condense out of the airstream.

It seems like overkill, but the air supply is what carries the paint (in most cases). If the air supply is loaded with moisture and impurities,

those impurities will show up in your finished paint job.

Starting at the compressor, connect a flexible hose to the main feed line. This will isolate the compressor's vibration so it does not cause cracks in the main feed line. The main feed line should be of either galvanized steel or copper and have an inner diameter of at least 3/4in. Like the compressor, a bigger main feed line is better than a small one. A bigger feed line will handle more air and effectively adds to the size of the compressor's storage tank. The main line should run downhill slightly, with a valve or clean-out at the far end.

It would be nice if we could run plastic pipe for the air distribution system because it is so much easier to cut and assemble. Unfortunately, the record on plastic pipe is mixed. I have heard horror stories of exploding plastic pipe, but I have also heard of two commercial shops in Kansas City that have used plastic pipe for many years. The key seems to be selecting piping with a high enough pressure rating and then isolating it from compressor vibration.

No matter what the air distribution material is, the branch lines off the main feeder line should

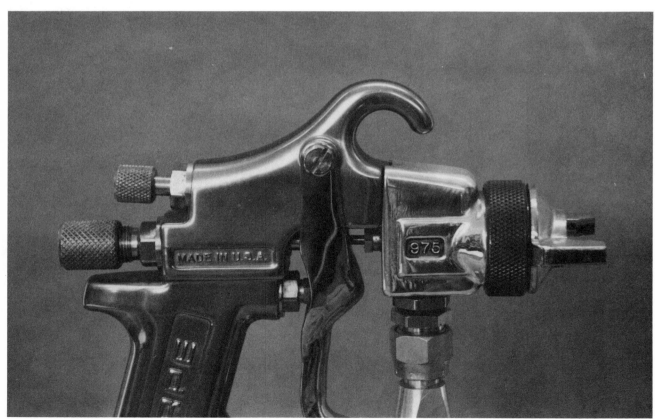

Most spray guns have two adjustments, fan shape and material. This Sharpe gun has the two "classic" adjustments. The lower knob controls the amount of material *(by controlling the trigger pull) while the upper knob controls the fan shape (by controlling the amount of air to the horns).*

16

run up and then turn and run down (check the illustration to relieve any confusion). This prevents any crud inside the main line from finding its way into the individual distribution lines. Keeping water out of your air supply involves more than just a large compressor and well-designed air lines. Moisture traps are available in a number of designs from simple little canisters that collect water in the bottom, to large stainless steel containers that hold a quart of water and include a pressure regulator.

There are two important things about these water traps. The most important is that you buy and install one, no matter which style you choose. The other important thing about water traps is their location. Most of us mount the trap right next to the compressor (it always seemed like a logical location to me). The trouble is that the air leaving the compressor is hot, thus any moisture will exist as a gas—fully absorbed by the airstream. A trap mounted further along the main feeder tube will trap much more water because the air at that point will have cooled, condensing the water out of the airstream.

I have borrowed more tips to this compressor business from the *PPG Refinish Manual* (a great book you can probably obtain from your paint jobber): Now that you have the expensive compressor, keep the oil clean, just like your Harley. When you service the compressor, be sure to clean the intake air filter. You might even want to mount the intake outside the building; this will reduce the noise and keep the filter cleaner for a much longer period. Finally, be sure to drain the air compressor's tank on a regular basis.

Spray Guns

Choosing a spray gun used to be a simple matter of matching your budget to the guns available. Once purchased, it was just a matter of learning to use the gun and keeping it clean. Like many things around us, the world of spray painting, and painting guns in particular, has changed in the last few years.

Of note, non-production (sometimes called light-duty) spray guns put out less material but their CFM requirements are much lower than a big production gun. Non-production guns are often well suited to situations where you are not painting large objects and where the compressor size is marginal.

The first effective spray gun was developed by a man named DeVilbiss during the Civil War. DeVilbiss discovered that a high-pressure stream of air passing through a tube would siphon liquid from a cup connected to the main air line by a smaller tube. DeVilbiss' goal in developing the first spray guns was to provide an effective means of spraying medicines and disinfectants during the

war; it was soon found that other liquids could be atomized and applied in this fashion.

Today, two types of spray guns exist: the standard siphon, or high-pressure gun, and the newer HVLP (high volume, low pressure). The standard siphon is over one hundred years old. Today's guns, manufactured by companies like DeVilbiss, Binks, Sharpe, and a dozen more, are far superior to anything Mr. DeVilbiss conceived, yet they remain a siphon gun with all the advantages and disadvantages of that basic design.

On the plus side of the ledger, the high-speed airstream (usually 40psi or more) does a good job of atomizing the paint and delivering it to the object being painted. On the minus side, however, that airstream moves the paint at high speed toward—but not always onto—the object being sprayed. Some of the paint misses the object entirely, some of it hits with such force that it bounces back into the air. Siphon guns get as little as 25 percent of the paint onto the car or motorcy-

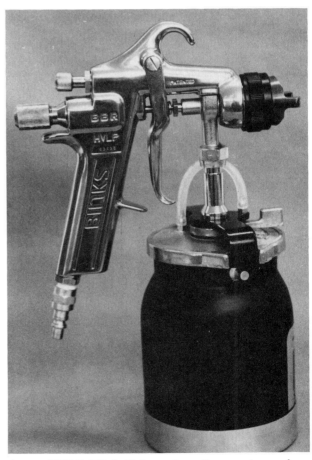

A new HVLP (High Volume Low Pressure) gun from Binks. These guns have been developed to ensure high transfer efficiencies and minimized air pollution. Quality HVLP guns will meet rule 1151 governing transfer efficiencies for Southern California.

cle. The rest of the paint, as well as the solvents mixed with the paint, go up in the air or on the walls of your shop.

The paint industry has a means of measuring the amount of material that actually goes on the fender, as opposed to the amount that goes in the atmosphere. Transfer efficiency (TE) is simply a measure of the amount of paint that is actually transferred from the gun to the object. As stated, siphon style guns commonly have a TE of only about 25 percent. The new HVLP guns, by contrast, have TEs of 75 percent and more.

By delivering roughly three times as much material to the object, the amount of paint used is dramatically reduced. This means lower material costs for painting, less overspray in the atmosphere (and on the walls of the shop), and less solvent usage (meaning reduced Volatile Organic Compounds, or VOCs, in the atmosphere). VOCs are a big issue, especially in areas like Southern California which has some of the worst air pollution in the United States. In fact, pollution is such an issue in the L.A. basin that the California South Coast Air Quality Management District came up with rule 1151. This ruling requires spray guns to meet minimum TE specifications as a means of limiting the amount of VOCs spewed into the air by body shops in the region. So far, the only guns to meet the strict standards are HVLP designs.

HVLP guns and systems atomize the paint with a high volume of low-pressure air, as opposed to the standard high-pressure siphon type gun which uses a small volume of high-pressure air to atomize the paint. The two basic types of HVLPs are turbine and compressor style.

Turbine systems use their own turbine style compressor to supply a large volume of air to the gun at a low (less than 10psi) pressure. Like most HVLP systems, these systems atomize and carry the paint with a high volume of low-pressure air. The turbine systems have a number of advantages. By separating the paint gun from the shop's compressor, it does not matter whether that compressor is 5hp or only 1hp. Also, the high-speed turbine blades tend to heat the air through rotational friction. This heated air expands in the turbine, thus reducing the relative humidity.

Most HVLP guns have the same adjustments as conventional spray guns, fan shape and material. The adjustments, however, might be in different locations. This Binks HVLP gun has the two adjustment knobs in the standard locations. When buying a new gun, it is important to get the right air nozzle, needle, and fluid nozzle (located in the gun just behind the air nozzle).

Because the turbine does little compressing, the air stays at a uniform temperature so problems with condensation in the air lines are minimized. Gone too are worries about the compressor picking up oil or contaminants from its own crankcase.

Some painters do not want the bother of another piece of equipment in the shop and for them there are HVLP guns that run off compressor air. These guns are able to convert the high-pressure compressor air to a low-pressure air—with more volume of course—inside the gun. The air leaving the gun measures less than 10psi. Unlike siphon guns, these guns pressurize the paint in the pot and use that pressure to bring the paint up to meet the airstream.

HVLP guns that run off the shop's compressor come in two distinct styles: those that use the compressor to supply all the air to the gun and those that supplement the compressor air with ambient air. The first type, using nothing but compressor air, has a large CFM requirement, meaning you need a serious compressor (probably 5hp). The sec-

ond type of HVLP gun runs off the compressor too, but is able to supplement that air with air from the shop. Basically, this second style uses a venturi in the gun to create a low-pressure area and siphon in surrounding air. The big advantage of such a system is the lowered compressor requirement. Instead of a requirement of 15 to 22 CFM, these guns only need 8 to 12 CFM.

Buying an HVLP gun or system is not the cheapest way to go. The 1993 Eastwood Company catalog offers their Accuspray HVLP turbine system for $669, while in another section of the same catalog a Binks standard spray gun is $145 plus the price of a cup. The company also offers an HVLP gun that runs off shop air for $449. These are neither the highest nor lowest costs for good spray equipment, rather they are representative of the prices and price differences you will find when shopping for equipment.

It might be tough to justify the extra expense of an HVLP system when a high-pressure siphon gun is so much less. Keeping the environment clean is a great concept, and the new HVLP equip-

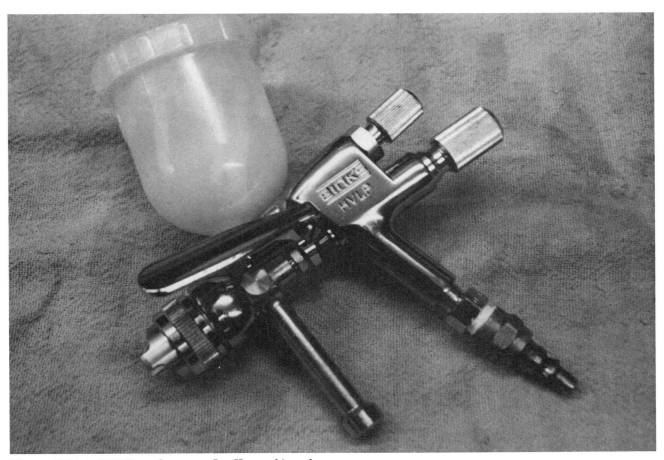

The small Binks HVLP touch-up gun Jon Kosmoski used for some of the work seen in this book. This gun offers the advantages of HVLP in a small package.

ment is already required in many parts of the country. But as an occasional painter, you might have a hard time parting with three times as much money based on environmental criteria alone.

Consider, then, the high cost of material (urethane paints can run as much as $150 per gallon) and the fact that an HVLP system will use much less paint. The other major consideration is the mess and fog created by siphon guns in a small shop. Working in your garage, there is never as much ventilation as you would like and there is usually more fog in the air than is healthy, even with the right mask and filters. Most HVLP sys-tems create less than half the overspray, meaning less chance to breathe the often toxic fumes and less clean up in the shop afterwards.

Anatomy of a Spray Gun
High-Pressure Siphon Type Gun

The modern high-pressure siphon type guns from Binks, DeVilbiss, Sharp, and others feature the same basic design. Essentially, air passing through the spray gun siphons paint from the can, which is usually incorporated into the design of the gun. The two-stage trigger controls both air and liquid—pulling the trigger back part way allows air to pass through the gun while pulling it back all the way allows liquid paint to be pulled from the cup. That liquid paint is introduced to the airstream at the point where the air is leaving the gun.

Paint and air both leave the gun at the air cap and immediately begin to mix. Atomization occurs in two or three stages, beginning when the fluid leaves the gun, surrounded by a column of air that leaves the gun from the ring surrounding the fluid

In addition to the traditional adjustments, a Mattson compressor-driven HVLP gun has an adjustable regulator to control the pressure to the gun and an optional gauge to measure the air pressure at the air cap.

An HVLP gun from Croix Air. The small tube puts pressure on the paint in the pot. The one-way valve prevents paint from discharging back into the gun at the wrong time.

20

nozzle tip. Most air caps have at least one more set of air ports near the fluid nozzle tip that provide additional air to the paint and air mixture as it leaves the gun. These additional ports provide secondary atomization. Most guns have small air ports in the "horns" of the air cap. These are used primarily to shape the paint mist, though the additional air serves to aid atomization of the paint.

Most spray guns of this type have two basic adjustments controlled by the two small knobs seen on the back of the gun. The top knob controls air to the horns of the air cap and is used to control the size of the paint fan. The lower knob controls the amount of fluid leaving the gun.

Before adjusting the gun to spray a nice pattern, choose the right air cap and fluid nozzle. Different materials require the use of different air caps and fluid nozzles and each set has a different CFM rating. Be sure to match the cap and fluid nozzle to both the material you are spraying and the capacity of your compressor.

When it comes to setting the adjustments on a new high-pressure gun, each painter seems to have his or her own formula. Painter Mallard Teal uses the basic adjustments he learned in trade school: "I screw both the material and fan adjust-

ments in all the way and then back out the top (or fan) adjustment three turns and the bottom (material) adjustment three-and-one-half turns." Jon Kosmoski follows a similar procedure, though he uses different adjustment settings. Kosmoski uses the gun with the top adjustment wide open and the material knob backed out about two turns.

When it comes to using a spray gun, there are a couple basic points with which everyone agrees: Follow the pressure recommendations set by the paint manufacturer, and try to use the lowest pressure that will give the desired pattern. Ultimately, the correct pressure is the one that yields the pattern you want. Finally, keep the gun clean. Gun manufacturer's (both high-pressure and HVLP) report that nearly all the complaints they receive can be traced to dirty equipment.

HVLP Guns

HVLP guns are similar to the high-pressure siphon guns in their basic anatomy. A one- or two-stage trigger controls fluid and usually the air flow as well. Most have a material control like a high-pressure gun, though not all have the conventional "air control" knob like a high-pressure gun. Some control the fan by either moving the air cap or adjusting a small knob located near the air cap. All

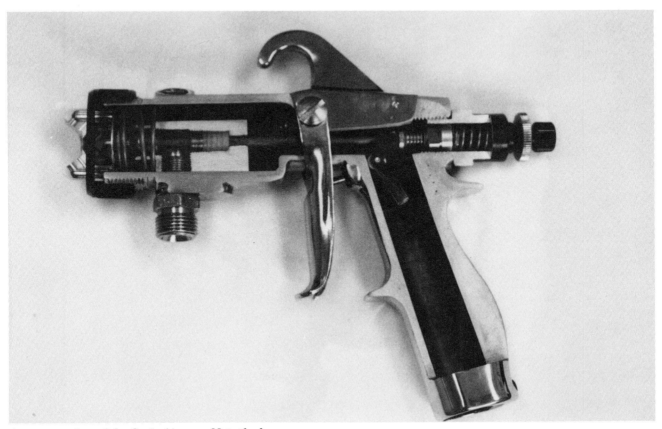

A cutaway view of the Croix Air gun. Note the large passages for the high volume of air at low pressure.

these guns, whether operated by a turbine or a compressor, apply pressure to the paint in the paint pot.

As is the case with high-pressure guns, the first step with your new HVLP system is to install the right air cap and fluid nozzle for the material at hand.

HVLP guns are not nearly as "universal" in their adjustments as the old high-pressure siphon style guns. However, they all pressurize the pot that holds the paint and they all have two basic adjustments, material and fan shape, though not always in the location of the traditional high-pressure guns.

Ron Durkin, a representative for Croix Air, recommends the following procedure when starting with one of their new guns:

1) Always turn the material control knob way down (clockwise as you hold the gun in this case) to eliminate the chance of starting out with too heavy a flow.

2) Set the fan to the neutral position. Each gun is different; for the Croix gun this means setting the air cap flush with the tip of the needle.

3) Set the air at the regulator (with a compressor style HVLP gun) at 40psi with the trigger pulled.

Working from these initial adjustments, Durkin recommends using a test panel to dial in the amount of material and the pattern that seems right for the job. He adds that there are two mistakes people who use an HVLP gun for the first time commonly make.

"If they're used to a siphon-style high-pressure gun," Durkin said, "then they put the material on too heavy, because they can't understand that even if the same amount of material is going through the gun, a lot more of it is actually coating the object being painted. They get the paint on way too thick, sometimes they get runs and sags as a result. The other mistake they make is holding the gun too far away from the material. The lower pressure airstream means that the air won't carry the paint as far, so you've got to get closer to the work, more like 6–8in instead of 8-10in."

How to Spray Paint in Ten Words or Less

When you decide to fire up that paint gun for the first time, remember the basics of spray painting. First, the gun must be moving when you pull the trigger and begin applying material. With a two-stage trigger, painters usually pull the trigger part way so air moves through the gun, start their hand moving, and then fully pull the trigger as the

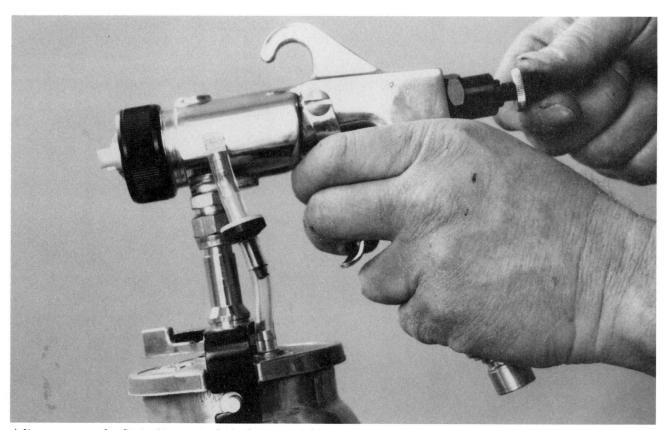

Adjustments on the Croix Air gun include this material knob, used to control the trigger pull.

Interview: Jim Bryntesen of Croix Air

Jim Bryntesen started selling HVLP equipment fifteen years ago, long before it was a buzz word in the automotive finishing industry. In the 1970s, Bryntesen sold Sicmo spray guns, a predecessor to today's Croix Air equipment, but his experience with HVLP equipment goes back even farther than that.

Where did HVLP painting start?

My first personal experience with HVLP was when my friend and I painted his Cushman scooter with the attachment on his mom's Hoover vacuum cleaner. Commercially HVLP started in Europe. I think the people over there were a little fussier in terms of transfer efficiency, the environment, and the health hazards of the overspray.

People in the aviation industry were the first to use HVLP because there's so much metal to paint and because there aren't many paint booths for aircraft. This means you really need a system that has high TE and doesn't put so much overspray in the air.

What are the inherent advantages of HVLP?

Well, of course they have very good transfer efficiency. But another big advantage is being able to spray on location. With conventional high-pressure systems, you need a big compressor and that means a 220-volt power supply. If you've got a turbine system, which runs off 110 volts, you are self-contained. It is great for painting contractors and people who work on the job site.

The turbine systems are easy for a rookie painter to use because they're spraying with hot air. They're a lot easier to use, you can put the paint on wet, it won't run or sag. The air leaving a high pressure gun at 65psi will measure 34 degrees. The cold air tends to retard evaporation of the solvents. Under the same conditions, a turbine will be putting out 100-degree air, so the turbine system will flash [begin to harden at the surface] the paint off quicker. Of course you've got to use a slower reducer, a lot of people don't understand that and the paint isn't mixed correctly.

Because we spray with low pressure air, there is less disturbance, less dirt and dust put up in the air by the spraying—so you've got a cleaner paint job. Big shops can slow down the air moving through the booth, so they need less heat and less electricity to run the ventilation fans.

There is always a cost. What are the disadvantages of turbine-style HVLP?

On large surfaces such as aircraft, it is noticeably slower than conventional spraying, though the paint savings will usually justify the extra labor. And it is more expensive to buy the equipment.

Why are some people reluctant to try HVLP?

At the body shop level, there's the cost of the equipment. A turbine system costs a lot more than a high-pressure gun. Even with non-turbine systems, the guns are more expensive than a high-pressure siphon gun.

In terms of day-to-day use, what are the differences between a turbine HVLP and one that runs off the compressor?

The turbine has the advantage of never having oil or water in the airstream. It has total portability, needing only 110 volts. And it is nice because of the hot air leaving the gun. In a situation where there's a need for a higher production rate, then a conversion HVLP gun works better than a turbine system.

What are typical CFM requirements for the various guns?

High-pressure siphon style guns need 8–10CFM. Some HVLP conversion guns need 15–22CFM, some of the paint people say 20CFM (4CFM per horsepower). With one of our venturi guns (a gun that runs off the compressor but supplements that air with ambient air), you need 8–12CFM.

Do all HVLP guns pressure-feed the pot?

Yes, they all put some pressure on the paint in the pot. The only exception is a few gravity feed guns with the pot mounted up above the gun handle.

Some painters say HVLP guns are okay, but that the guns won't work with metallics or pearls. What do you say?

Remember that not all HVLP guns are the same. Some of the HVLP guns that run off the compressor are really just high-pressure guns that have been "converted" to HVLP use. The trouble is that the air passages inside the gun aren't big enough to work with the larger volumes of low pressure air in-

Jim Bryntesen from Croix Air has been selling and using HVLP guns since he and a friend painted a motor scooter with a Hoover vacuum-cleaner spray gun.

side a good HVLP gun. What I'm trying to say is that a good HVLP gun will spray metallics just fine, but only a good one.

There are many new HVLP guns on the market. How does a person buy a good one?

A good HVLP must move air, it has to have a full body with big enough passages. It can't be a little skinny high-pressure look-alike. If you are buying a turbine system, make sure it has a good air filter. Remember the air you are spraying with is only as clean as the rating of the filter. Avoid rubber and plastic O-rings in the gun because they are attacked by the chemicals in the paint thinners.

Buy from a supplier who understands the equipment. Buy direct if you can, from someone who really understands the equipment so you can get some good advice as to which nozzles to run and how to use the equipment.

Where do first-time HVLP users get in trouble?

They use too fast a solvent. With turbine or compressor HVLP guns, the air is warmer and there's a high volume so you need a slower solvent.

You also need to keep the gun closer to the object, 6–8in instead of 8–10in.

Compressor-operated guns need a larger air hose. If you use anything smaller than 5/16in ID you are in trouble and won't get enough air even with a big air compressor. Three-eighths inch hose would be even better.

A compressor driven HVLP gun really needs good moisture and oil traps because you are moving a lot of air.

A lot of these systems are sold by jobbers and supply houses that are used to selling high-pressure guns. So no one knows what size needle and cap to use with HVLP guns. Everybody knows what size tip a high-pressure gun needs, but HVLP is so new that no one knows what to use for needle and air cap.

It comes back to making sure you buy direct or from a jobber or supplier who really understands the system and can help out a little in setting up the gun with the proper fluid set. Croix, for example, runs an 800 phone number to answer any technical questions.

gun approaches the area where they need to start painting.

Second, always keep the gun at 90 degrees to the object being painted. That way the paint goes on evenly. If the gun is tipped relative to the ob-

ject, the top or bottom of the paint fan will contain more paint than the other.

Third, always move the gun in straight lines across the object (for more on gun handling, see the Jon Kosmoski interview in the next section).

Croix Air uses an adjustable air cap to control the size and shape of the paint fan. Note that the air cap is num- *bered. Air cap, needle, and fluid nozzle must be matched and correctly chosen for the material you intend to spray.*

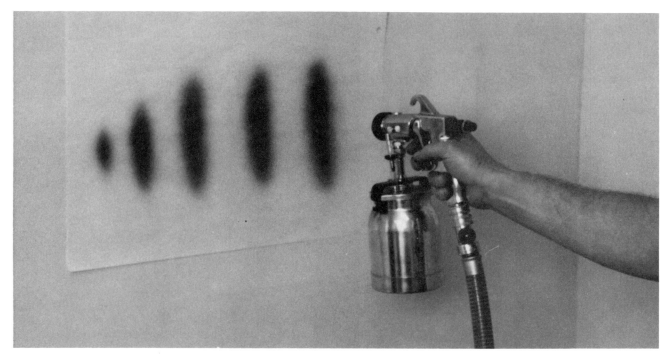

A graphic demonstration of the differences in fan shape available with the Croix gun (and most others).

Each pass of the gun must be parallel to the last regardless of the shape of the object being painted. An object that combines flat panels with curves (think of a rectangular one-gallon can of lacquer thinner) will require that the flat panels be painted in a series of horizontal passes across each panel, combined with a "banding" pass up or down the curved section at the corner.

Fourth, unless the paint manufacturer tells you otherwise, each pass of the gun (as you work across a flat panel for example) should overlap the last pass by 50 percent.

Shop Safety

Safety is the dullest part of most technical books and the one section too many people skip over. The following comments regarding your safety in the shop have been kept short—in the hope that more readers will actually read them instead of skipping to the next section for some "real" information.

We tend to avoid safety warnings in the belief that we are too tough or that nothing bad can happen to us. The new miracle paints are better than ever, but part of the miracle has been achieved at considerable cost—cost in the form of high toxicity. Whether you paint once a year or once a week, the chemicals can and will hurt you if you do not take the proper precautions.

The materials you need protection from include dust, paint, and solvent in both vapor and

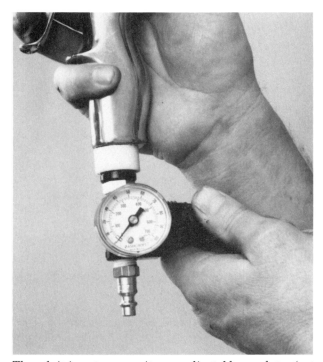

Though it is not a necessity, an adjustable regulator (not an air restriction valve) makes it convenient to adjust the pressure at the gun and means you do not have to compensate for any pressure loss in a long air hose. The small, white band above the fitting is the filter where this Croix Air gun picks up ambient air to supplement the compressor air.

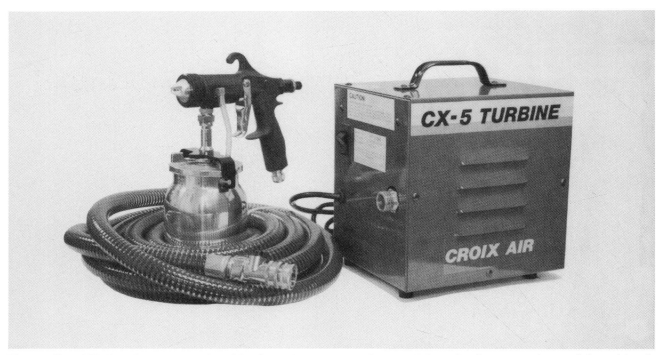

The smallest HVLP turbine set up offered by Croix Air. At $495 (sometimes less) it is reasonably priced and well suited to painting small objects—like motorcycle parts. A turbine HVLP outfit eliminates the need for a big air compressor and minimizes condensation problems as well.

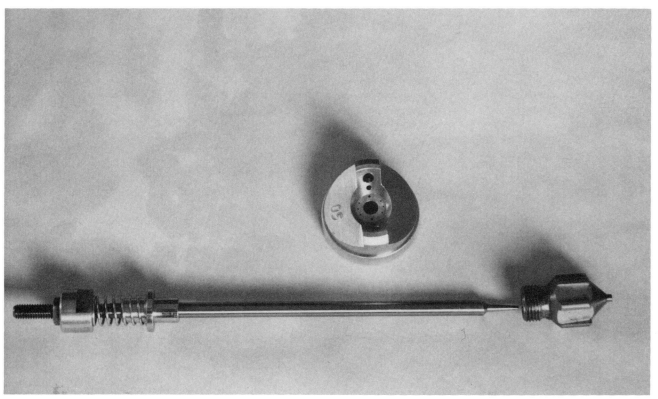

Sometimes called the fluid set, this is the air nozzle (or air cap), fluid nozzle, and needle assembly. When you buy a spray gun—either HVLP or conventional—be sure these three parts are matched to the material and pressures you intend to use.

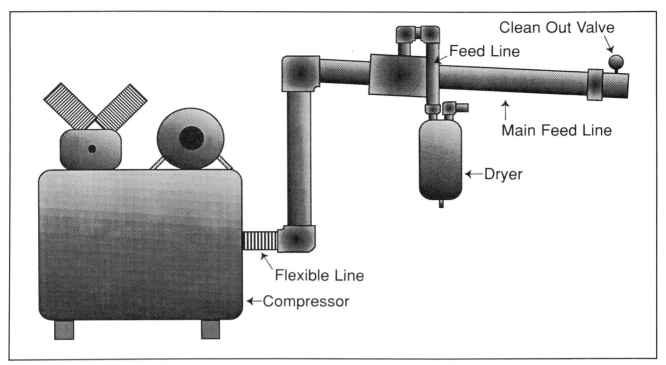

A good air supply starts with a compressor of at least 3hp, preferably 5hp. A flexible line between the compressor and the feed line will prevent vibration from cracking the line. The main feed line should be large, at least 3/4in inner diameter. Junctions run up before turning *down to prevent the entry of dirt and moisture into the spray gun or air tool. Note that the main feed line runs downhill slightly and has a clean-out valve at the end. Dryers are more effective when they are placed as far from the compressor as possible.*

liquid form, and the isocyanate based materials in both liquid and vapor form.

To protect yourself from sanding dust, always wear at least a good dust filter and eye protection. Goggles will protect your eyes from flying debris and also prevent vapors from being absorbed by the mucous membranes around your eyes.

The next step in protection would be a charcoal type respirator of the type used in all painting operations that do not involve isocyanates. You also need eye protection, either in the form of goggles or a full-face respirator that integrates eye protection. Many painters wear special coveralls and rubber gloves during any painting operations. These protect the wearer from chemicals entering through the skin. The overalls also prevent your flannel shirt from contributing lint to the new paint job.

For spraying urethanes or any paints containing the dread isocyanates—especially in a non-paint booth atmosphere where the ventilation is poor—you need a hood or full mask supplied with fresh air from its own compressor. This equipment can be rented from many large rental companies so you do not have to pay out the big bucks on equipment that only gets occasional use.

Just a few more tips before closing. Do not use solvents and thinners to wash your hands or remove paint from hands and arms. Chemicals in the liquids are absorbed through the skin and end up in your blood stream. Use waterless hand cleaner or a similar product.

Finally, as you spend hundreds of dollars outfitting your garage, spend just a few more and buy at least one good fire extinguisher, designed to handle chemical fires, and a smoke detector.

Understanding Modern Paints

What All Those Labels Mean

In the days when Harleys were either Knuckles or Panheads, choosing a paint was a simple matter. There were enamels and nitrocellulose lacquers in a limited range of colors. Today, there are at least three types of finish paints in a bewildering array of colors, not to mention special finishes like metallics, pearls, and candy colors. Making sense of all this is easier if we first break the paint down

The two parts of the two-part primer from House of Kolor. Unlike many two-part primers, this can be used as a primer-surfacer. House of Kolor

to its basic components, and then discuss the three types of paint available.

Inside the Paint Can

Paint, any paint, is made up of three components: pigment, resin, and solvent, as well as a few additives.

Pigment is the material that gives paint its color. Older paints often used lead-based pigments while modern paints have converted to nonlead pigments. One of the challenges for modern paint chemists has been finding new nontoxic pigments to take the place of the older lead-based materials.

Resin (also known as binder) helps to hold the pigments together and keep them sticking to the metal. Solvent is the carrier used to make the paint thin enough to spray. In the case of lacquers, a true thinner is used. In the case of enamels, the solvent is a reducer.

Additives are materials added to the paint to give it a certain property or help it overcome a problem, much the same way additives are incorporated into modern oils to improve their performance.

If we are going to talk about paint, there are a few more terms to get out of the way. One that crops up more and more these days is Volatile Organic Compounds (VOCs). Another related term is "solids," as in high-solids paint.

The solvent (a volatile material) evaporates (or oxidizes) after the paint is sprayed on the bike, leaving behind the pigment and binder, known as the solids. Solvents that evaporate into the atmosphere are known in the industry as VOCs and have come under government regulation in areas like Southern California and New York City. These VOCs react with sunlight and can be a major contributor to smog.

Paint manufacturers are trying to increase the percentage of solids in their paints in order to reduce the amount of solvent and thus the VOC emissions. In the case of sandable primers, high-solids mean that the primer contains a high percentage of solids and that these solids can be used to fill scratches and small imperfections in the surface (see the "Primer" and Primer Surfaces" section later in this chapter for more information).

Three Types of Paint

Most of the paints available for painting your Harley can be classified as either enamel, lacquer, or urethane. Though urethanes are technically an enamel, they will be considered as a separate type of paint.

Enamel

Enamels have been used to cover everything from Fords to Frigidaires. Most modern enamels are acrylic enamels (meaning they contain plastic), offering better flexibility and durability than the older alkyd enamel. Many modern enamel paints can be catalyzed with isocyanate, which aids cross-linking of the paint molecules thus improving the durability of the finish.

Enamel uses a reducer instead of a thinner as the solvent part of the mix. An enamel paint job hardens as the reducer evaporates and the resin oxidizes (mixes with oxygen). You might not give a darn about evaporation or oxidation until you realize that the need for oxidation adds considerably to the drying time of an enamel paint job.

Acrylic enamel makes a fine finish though most custom painters shy away from the material because the long drying time means more time for dust to be trapped on the surface of the paint and more time to wait to apply second coats or tape-out a design. You will find too that most of what we call "custom" paints are available as either an acrylic lacquer or urethane.

Lacquer

Lacquer paints have been available for years and years. During the early 1950s, most of the custom cars and bikes were painted with lacquer—nitrocellulose lacquer to be exact. This early lacquer

This UFC-1 urethane clear from House of Kolor is catalyzed with isocyanates and requires the use of a fresh-air hood during any spraying. House of Kolor

was easy to work with and offered some vibrant colors but had at least two major drawbacks. First, nitrocellulose is a toxic material and second, those early lacquer paint jobs tended to crack with age due to the paint's inability to flex. By the late 1950s, everyone had switched to a new lacquer formula—acrylic lacquer. This new material eliminated the toxic nitrocellulose while the addition of the acrylic provided better resistance to ultraviolet radiation and also gave the paint more flexibility.

This neon base coat from House of Kolor is extremely bright—though it fades with exposure to the sun. Like all the House of Kolor base coats, this material can be covered with either lacquer or urethane clear coats. House of Kolor

The increased flexibility helped to eliminate most of the cracking that occurred with the earlier material. Custom painters have always liked lacquer because of its fast drying time, low toxicity (for the acrylic lacquers), great color, and the ease with which spot repairs can be made. Custom painters often put on lacquer in multiple coats, wet sanding between coats. The end result is a deep shine that you can almost swim in and a perfectly smooth surface created by sanding between coats.

The trouble with acrylic lacquer is its lack of durability (it chips and stains fairly easily) and the

These pearl base coats from House of Kolor are usually sprayed over a white base coat to enhance the glow of the pearl. Again, these can be covered with either lacquer or urethane clear coats. House of Kolor

Candy colors from House of Kolor are available in either urethane or lacquer. To paraphrase Mark Twain: The reports of lacquer's death have been greatly exaggerated. Expect to see lacquer in most parts of the country for another ten years. House of Kolor

Your local Harley-Davidson dealer has a variety of paints for sale. Touch-up paint to match your late-model Harley is available in either spray cans or small brush-in-bottles. For a complete paint job, original colors are available by the quart.

large amount of maintenance a lacquer paint job requires. The great lacquer shine comes only after plenty of wet sanding and polishing. Keeping the paint looking good means regular sessions with polish and wax.

The other problem with lacquer paints is the VOC issue discussed earlier. The evaporating thinner and the multiple coats (more thinner) means that spraying lacquer puts a relatively large amount of VOCs in the atmosphere. People within the industry predict that the day will come when lacquer will no longer be available, though no one seems to know exactly when that will be.

Urethane

The hot stuff in the custom painting field is urethane. What's urethane? Technically, it is an enamel, yet it sprays much like a lacquer. Urethane is a relatively new two-part paint material catalyzed with isocyanate. Even though it is classed as an enamel, urethane dries fast and offers easy spot repairs. The fast drying means quick application of second coats, easy candy paint jobs and fast tape-outs for flame jobs and graphics. Unlike lacquer, urethane is super durable, resisting rock chips and chemical stains better than anything except powder coating.

Urethane can be used in a base coat, clear coat situation or as a one-shot application. Because of its durability, urethanes are a good choice for frames, wheels, and engine cases.

The biggest single downside to the urethane paints is the toxicity of the catalyst, the isocyanates. These materials are so toxic that spraying with urethanes requires a fresh-air system (especially in home painting situations where ventilation is limited) so that the painter is sure to breathe absolutely no shop air. The other downside to urethanes is their higher cost.

Custom Paints

Custom paint jobs are often applied in multiple layers. The first finish coat is called the base coat. This base layer of paint can be any color or a metallic paint. The base coat can be covered by a candy coat or a clear coat.

Candy colors were discovered in the 1950s when custom painters like Jon Kosmoski tried putting a little tint in a can of clear and then spraying the tinted clear over the base color. The final color in a candy paint job is a combination of the base color as seen through the tinted coat on top. The effect was much like looking through a piece of translucent colored candy. These new candy paint jobs became the hot ticket for both custom bikes and cars and remain so to this day. By combining different base coats with different candy colors (and a different number of candy coats), an infinite number of colors are possible.

Sometimes the base coat is simply covered with a clear coat. Clear coats have become com-

Custom Painting Techniques

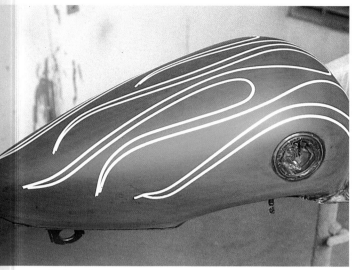

Before the tape out, Jon Kosmoski scuffed this tank with 500-grit sandpaper and wiped it down with wax and grease remover. Jon does the actual designing on the tank using thin masking tape. In this case, he decided to use long flowing flames that do not crisscross. A small ruler can be used to ensure that the flames are in the same position on both sides.

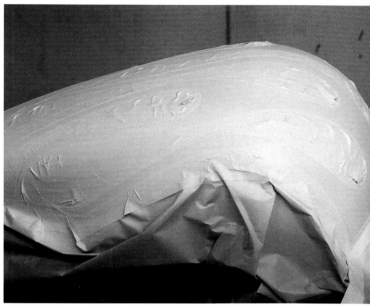

After wiping the tank with a tack rag, Jon sprays on two coats of the white base coat from his House of Kolor paint line. These urethane base coats dry quickly, making it easy to do a multi-colored job like this one.

After the initial design, the rest of the tank is taped off with 3/4in masking tape. Always use brand name tape and make sure it sticks well or the paint will creep under the edges. At this point you can see the design of the flames—do not be afraid to pull the tape and start over if it does not look right (wipe off the tape residue if you do pull the tape). The two sides of the tank (or tanks) do not have to be exactly the same because no one can see both sides at once—but be sure the top (or tops) are the same.

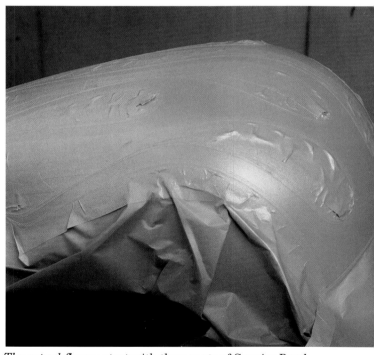

The actual flames start with three coats of Sunrise Pearl applied to the front of the tank. Each coat must flash before applying the next. As always, Jon stresses the importance of sufficient air movement in the shop and a minimum temperature of 70 degrees.

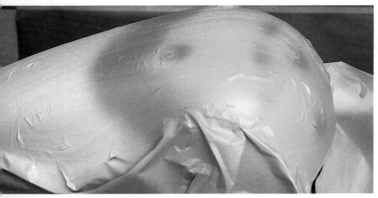

A slightly darker color, Tangelo Pearl, is applied farther back on each flame lick and at the area that separates the front of each flame. Jon applied three coats, blending the area where the Tangelo meets the Sunrise.

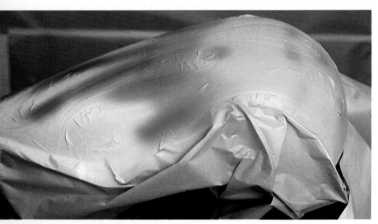

Now this is starting to look good. Hot Pink Pearl is the next color added to each flame lick, with Lavender Pearl at the ends. Paint must be applied from two angles for complete coverage next to the tape.

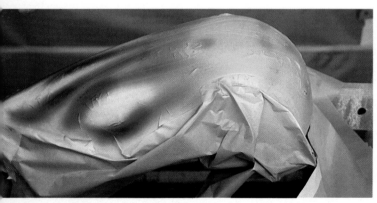

The gun is a HVLP touch-up gun; it puts out a nice, small pattern that works well for a job like this one. Blending the colors where they meet is an art and something you will need to practice. John blends the colors by using light coats and painting in only one direction at the point where the colors meet.

You can't really see what you have until the tape is pulled. Pull it right away to lessen the odds of pulling paint along with the tape. Jon puts the tape on in layers so it pulls off in large sections (easier than pulling each little piece one at a time). When possible, pull it away from the paint surface to avoid lifting the paint.

The next step is three (one tack and two medium) coats of clear. The pinstriping will be done on this clear coat. After the clear has dried, it is sanded with 500-grit paper to give the striping something to stick to. Many base coats go on flat and get their shine from the clear coat.

The final product. After pinstriping the tanks with his light blue urethane striping paint, Jon puts on two coats of clear, sands lightly, and then applies the final two coats of clear.

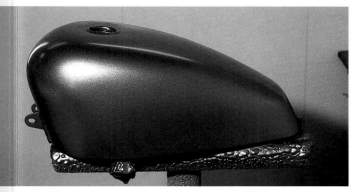

The Sportster tank seen in Chapter 7 after the first two coats of base coat. These materials are from the PPG line; the color is Pace Car blue, a Blue metallic base coat. A subtle two-tone effect will be created with two different base coats.

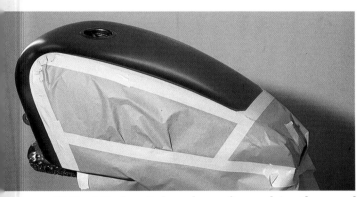

Mallard Teal waited one hour after applying the second coat of Pace Car Blue and then taped off a simple pattern on the tank. How long you wait before doing a tape out will depend on the individual paint product. It is important to follow the time recommendations for each type of paint.

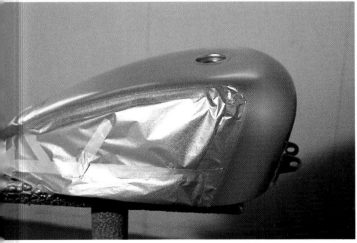

Our Sportster tank after two coats of Sterling Silver base coat. This is a simple silver metallic base coat from PPG.

The tape is pulled right away, revealing a two-toned tank. After the candy paint is applied, however, the two-tone effect will be subdued.

Illuminated by the camera's flash unit, the tank looks mostly blue with plenty of metallic showing through the three coats of Candy Cobalt Blue (from PPG). Each coat of candy makes the color darker and minimizes the difference between the two base coats.

The finished product. After three coats of Cobalt Blue, Mallard put on one good clear coat and sanded that with 600 grit. Next, Brian Truesdell put on the pinstripes, then Mallard applied the final clear coats and polished everything to a high luster. In sunlight, the metallic shows through and the bike appears to be one color. In soft light, little metallic shows through but there is a much more pronounced two-tone effect.

Custom Paint Gallery

Paul Shadley's FXR started as a ground-up restoration. The FXR frame received a new front section and a hand-made swingarm. Spoked wheels measure 21in in front and 16in in the rear.

Covering Paul's gas tank is an extra elegant paint job—the result of some collaboration between Dave Perewitz and Roy Mason. Dave sprayed the deep blue with crimson highlights using House of Kolor products, while Roy applied the gold leaf and the lettering on the tank. The final step was the multiple clear coats to create a smooth surface and protect the elaborate paint work.

The radical Softail, Wicked, Mean, Green, and Nasty. Note the fender rails, dash, license mount, and painted windshield—to mention just a few unusual features.

Green was long a taboo color for bikes, but no more. This lime green color and modern blue-and-white graphics make this bike jump! The blue and green have just enough contrast to make each stand out without clashing.

Paul Erpenbeck is a painter by trade—and it shows in his FXR. This is a good example of a simple bike that uses a few key parts and a good paint job for a great effect. Paul describes the bike as a "performance look and function on a budget." The Harley-Davidson racing colors and bold layout give the bike a look all its own.

Paul started his paint job with a white base coat (PPG materials) covered in clear mixed with White Pearl flakes. Next, he put down the red stripe followed by the black. The lettering was designed on a computer and cut on a plotter—Paul used the computer generated mask to spray through. Finally, everything got a coat of clear, a light sanding to knock down the edges, and more clear for a perfectly smooth paint job.

Mallard's bike seen in Chapter 8. To say that the aqua scallops on a purple base makes for a strong color combination is an understatement. The strong combination of rich colors and perfect luster give this bike great visual impact.

Next page
A close-up of the Purple Velvet tinted with Romanesque Crimson and the scallops done in Light Aqua tinted with Grandeur Blue. The black shadows and great pinstriping help to make the scallops stand out. Brian Truesdell did the pinstripes—note the two colors and how well each works.

40

mon on new cars and provide good protection from both ultraviolet rays and harsh chemicals; they provide a great shine, too. Some of the base coats dry with a flat finish, because the clear coat provides the shine.

Most modern candy paint jobs contain three distinct layers of paint. The base coat, (often a metallic or semi-metallic color) followed by the candy or tinted clear, and then topped by a clear coat for a great shine and good resistance to ultraviolet rays.

Most of us are familiar with metallic paint jobs. Tiny pieces of aluminum or other metals are added to the paint by the manufacturer or the painter to provide extra sparkle. Metallics are currently available from a number of suppliers in both silver and gold finishes, and in a number of sizes.

While metallics add sparkle to a paint job, pearls add a more subtle glow in much the same way. Pearl particles are tiny bits of synthetic material added to the paint. The glow of a pearl job comes from the light that strikes the pearl flakes and is then reflected to the viewer. The actual color you see depends on the color of the pearl particles, often acting in combination with the color of the base coat or the tinted clear coat.

Pearl paint jobs often react differently to different types and angles of light. Walking around a pearl job can be a little unsettling. From one direction you might see the blue base coat while from another you see the violet color reflected by the colored pearl chips. A good pearl job has a lovely soft glow almost as though the light is shining through the paint from underneath.

Polish

Though it is not a paint at all, anyone who intends to paint will need to know something about polish. In spite of our best efforts, many paint jobs come out of the garage with small imperfections in the top layer of paint or the final clear coat.

As a general rule, you should never sand or rub a candy color or a pearl. These paints are covered with a clear coat and any sanding or polishing is done to that clear coat. A number of paint-care companies have products or an entire system of products intended for polishing paint. Well known for their car-care products, the Meguiar's company has paint-care products available in auto and motorcycle shops. The number of products in either their professional or amateur lines is mind-boggling.

One question that crops up during any discussion of polishing is the use of a power buffer. A Meguiar's representative reports, "Most of our products work better with a power buffer, but when a person—especially an amateur—is in doubt about whether or not to use power, the answer is to do it by hand." Meguiar's also makes a

set of special buffing tools and accessories for use with their specific products.

Meguiar's recommends that you start the polishing with wet, 2000-grit sandpaper (if the imperfections are minor you could skip the sandpaper and start with the liquid polish). The next step is their number two liquid cleaner from their professional line, followed by their number nine fine-cut polish, followed by a good carnauba wax. Remember, it is easy to rub through, especially at any kind of edge, even when you are working by hand. Use a cotton towel (no wool pads or towels) large enough to fit the palm of your hand and be careful to stay away from any edges or raised areas. Remember too that urethane clear is a much tougher film than lacquer and rub accordingly.

Primer and Primer Surfaces

The finest candy paint job in the world will not last long if the preparation and materials used under the finish paint are not of the highest quality. First-time painters often think primer is just

Pinstriping requires some special materials. Most stripers use one of three available paints: One Shot Sign Painter's lettering enamel, urethane striping enamel from House of Kolor, or Chromatic lettering enamel.

If you want some extra glitter, purchase metal flakes in the raw and add them to the paint. Flakes are available in a variety of sizes, materials, and colors from any good paint supply store.

primer. Wrong. Primer comes in lacquer and two-part (often known as epoxy primer), as a sealer and as a primer-surfacer.

Wax and Grease Removers

Wax and grease remover is not even a paint, yet it is the first thing you should use on the surface before applying any kind of paint. If it ain't clean, the paint won't stick—period.

Metal Prep

If you have stripped the tanks and fenders to their birthday suits, you probably need to use a metal etch before spraying the first coat of primer. The metal etch prepares the bare metal for that first coat of paint. Though many shops spray epoxy primer over bare steel, many paint manufacturers recommend you treat the steel with metal etch first. Think of it as a primer for the primer.

Primer

A true primer is a paint material chosen for its good adhesion to the material it is sprayed over. Most provide good resistance to corrosion and moisture. A true primer is not meant to be sanded and contains a low percentage of solids.

Primer-Surfacer

Primer-surfacers are primer materials with a high solids content. While offering good adhesion like a straight primer, a primer-surfacer also helps fill small scratches and imperfections, and sands easily. Primer-surfacers should be applied in two or three thin coats and then sanded when dry. If you fail to allow the material to dry properly before sanding, it will shrink *after* you've finished sanding, allowing small scratches (known as sand scratches) to show through the finish paint job.

Epoxy Primer

An epoxy (or two-part) primer like DP 40 from PPG or EP-2 from House of Kolor is a more durable and expensive primer material. These materials are known for their superior bonding abilities and great corrosion resistance. An epoxy primer is a good choice for motorcycle gas tanks, and will help prevent spilled gasoline from working under the top coat of paint and causing a blister around the fill cap. The catalyst in these paints (at least in the case of PPG's and House of Kolor's products) is not an isocyanate so most painters spray these materials with only a charcoal type respirator. It should be noted that PPG recommends a fresh-air hood in spite of the fact that there are no isocyanates in these products.

Some of these, like the EP-2 and KP-2 from House of Kolor, can be sanded like a primer-surfacer, while others are meant to be used as a strict primer. Many of these can be used as the sealer coat before the color coats are applied. Though they are durable and useful materials, each is a little different so be sure to check the manufacturer's recommendations.

Primer-Sealer

A primer-sealer, sometimes known as a sealer, is meant to seal or separate two different layers of paint. A coat of sealer is often applied as the final coat of "primer" before starting with the first of the finish coats. This is not a sandable finish, but is meant to seal two different types of paint. For example, lacquer sprayed over enamel will often cause a reaction between the two paints, so a sealer is applied before the lacquer is applied. (Enamel sprayed over lacquer is not usually a problem but a sealer should be used anyway.)

The other advantage of using a primer-sealer is to achieve good color hold-out. Sometimes the final coat (or coats) of paint will soak into the primer coats underneath. This dulls and changes the color of the final coat. Color hold-out means the top or final coats are "held out" and prevented from mixing in any way with the paint underneath. This means the Porsche Guards Red you spray on the tanks will look like and remain looking like the color chip in the paint book.

Adhesion Promoter

Adhesion promoters are similar in intent to primer-sealers and are sometimes used to ensure that one coat of paint will stick to the older paint underneath.

Paint Compatibility

As stated earlier, it is dangerous to spray lacquer over enamel, less so to spray enamel over lacquer. You may wonder whether the paint on your Harley is lacquer or not. Well, just take a little lacquer thinner to a hidden spot and see if it dissolves the paint. Before spraying over an old paint job, remember that you not only must remember what type of paint works with another type, but also remember that you can only put the paint on so thick before it starts to crack, no matter what type of paint it is. If the old paint looks thick and shows any cracks, then it is probably already too thick. Jon Kosmoski feels that the modern lacquer jobs that crack do so simply because the paint is too thick.

So what all this means is that when in doubt about whether or not to put more layers over an old paint job there is one simple answer: Don't. Strip the paint and start fresh. In the case of a

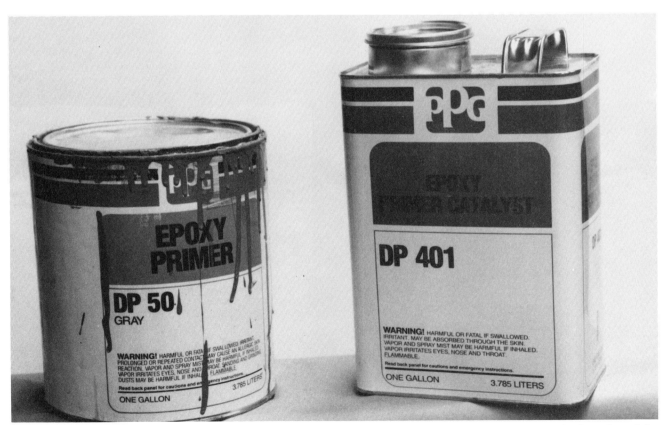

PPG makes its two-part primers in a variety of colors. This DP 50 is gray, while DP 40 is gray-green, 74 is red, and 90 is black. The idea is to match the color of the primer to the color of the topcoat.

1959 Cadillac, stripping the paint may not be an option. But a motorcycle, even a dresser (be careful with the fiberglass bags), is not so large that stripping the paint is out of the question.

By stripping the paint, you eliminate all the hassles of compatibility and too many layers of paint. By working from bare metal, you control all the steps in the painting process and are better able to ensure success. You will discover and eliminate any old body work and start over fresh. By discovering and repairing imperfections, you eliminate one more thing that might ruin your new paint job.

And Finally

The new paints are better than ever. They are more durable and colorful than anything seen before. There are, of course, just a few things to keep in mind.

Meguiar's makes a variety of paint-care products for use by professionals (shown) and nonprofessionals. Non-professional products tend to be easier to use. Their number nine is classified as a cleaner-polish, and can be used by hand to eliminate swirl marks or light oxidation. This product is often used in combination with 2000-grit sandpaper and their number two fine-cut cleaner to rub out fresh clear coats.

Manufacturers include information sheets for each product. These sheets contain a wealth of information regarding the mixing, use, and application of the paint. Should you follow one light coat with a heavy coat? How long are the flash times? When can you apply or remove tape? All these questions and more are answered in the product information sheets.

Strangely, safety information is not included in most of these information sheets, so you must rely on the paint can labels or ask for each product's Material Safety Data Sheet.

Speaking of safety, be sure to use a charcoal-type respirator in any painting situation, except where isocyanates are involved. When using isocyanates, use a separate fresh-air system. More safety is covered in Chapter 2.

Most modern paints have evolved into "systems" designed by each manufacturer to answer a certain need. Once you have decided which type of paint job you are going to apply, try to stick with one type of paint from one manufacturer. If you are spraying acrylic lacquer, use lacquer for the base, candy, and clear coat. By using one manufacturer, you know all the paints are designed to work together and be compatible.

If you have any questions about compatibility, be sure to ask the paint supplier. There is nothing worse than slaving over a great paint job only to have the paint wrinkle when you spray on the clear coat. Though primers and sealers are universal, never use one company's catalyst with another company's urethane paint.

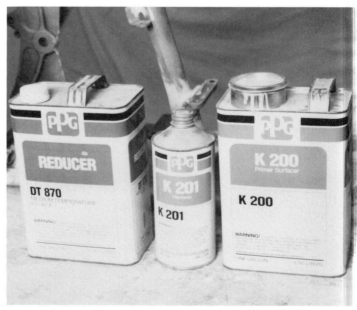

PPG makes a full line of primer and paints. This K 200 is a primer-surfacer, designed to build fast, fill small scratches and imperfections, and be easy to sand.

44

Professional painters sometimes cheat and put a particular urethane clear over an acrylic lacquer candy job. It works fine for them, but it is just not a good idea for the rest of us.

Both House of Kolor and PPG make base coats that contain no isocyanates and can be cleared with either urethane or lacquer. By clearing these paints with lacquer, you can do a paint job at home that is free of any isocyanates and requires no renting or buying of a fresh air system.

In order to do a successful paint job, you need to remember a few key rules of the painted road: Be careful with the preparation, use one type of paint from one manufacturer whenever possible, keep the shop at least 70 degrees, and read the directions *before* you start painting.

You can use most Meguiar's products either by hand or machine. For machine buffing, they make this two-part kit, with one pad for cutting and one for final polishing.

When using power buffers, it is important to keep the speed low and avoid rubbing through at the edges.

Chapter 4

Dents and Scratches

How to Make Them Disappear

Although it has been said before, we'll say it again: Quality preparation is the single most important thing you can do to ensure a good-looking paint job.

Although surface preparation is discussed in other chapters, the intent here is to explain how to prepare a less than ideal metal surface for paint. What do you do with that tank or fender that has a series of dings? How about the dented tank from

the day the asphalt got hot, the kickstand sank in, and the bike went over? No matter how careful you are, any bike that gets ridden is subject to a certain amount of wear and tear. By understanding how to confront a dent, you will be able to repair those little affirmations of Murphy's Law. Being able to repair a dent also means you can score good deals at swap meets by buying dented components that no one else wants.

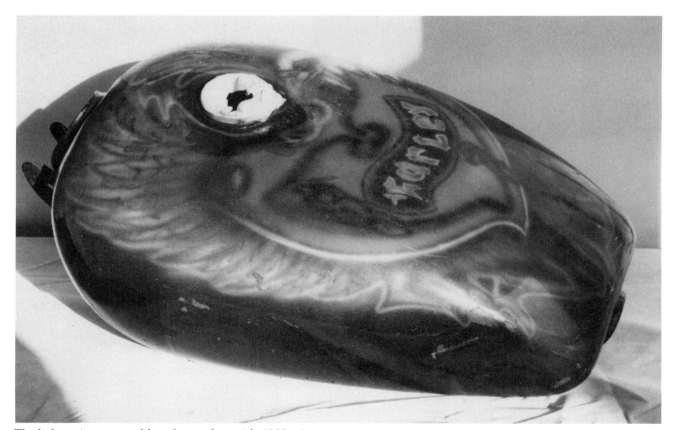

The before picture, an old tank complete with 1960s-vintage mural and a dent in its lower left corner.

Anatomy of a Dent

To you, a dented tank or fender might look like some smashed piece of metal; but to the trained eye, every dent has a specific anatomy. Much the way a doctor might examine a broken arm, a person trained in body repair examines a dent with an eye toward undoing the damage by unlocking the tension in the metal.

Upon closer inspection, a dent is usually a series of creases. If you were to cut a dented part in half, you would find the dent looks a bit like a cross-section taken from a mountain range. The peaks and valleys represent the creases put there during the impact. These creases are the key to understanding and repairing a dent. The creases contain the tension that holds the shape of the dent. You cannot get rid of the dent unless you relieve the tension contained in these V-shaped creases. Gordy Larson, a body and fender man for almost twenty years explained: "The dent is V-locked; the shape is locked up in that sharp V. You can't work out the dent unless you unlock the tension in the V-locks."

To oversimplify, when fixing a dent the idea is to knock down the peaks with a hammer and then work up the valleys with a hammer, a hammer and dolly, or a body pick. Remember that most manufacturer's do not want their body filler applied any more than 1/4in thick. So if you have a deep dent in a tank or fender, you cannot slop on the mud and fix it that way. Work out as much of the dent as possible with hammers and dollies before opening the can of filler.

In the real world, there are dents, especially in gas tanks, that cannot be successfully unlocked be- cause you cannot get at the back side to unlock the valley. In those cases, either put the filler on as thick as needed and hope for the best, or find a new or used tank.

Fill 'er Up? Body Fillers and Spot Putties

Once the dent has been worked as smooth as possible, you must fill the remainder of it with body filler. Everyone knows about plastic filler (often known as bondo), or at least they think they do. In reality, there are at least three types of plastic body filler: basic, lightweight, and stain free.

Basic body filler is a polyester plastic combined with a cream hardener. Sold by numerous companies under a variety of trade names, this basic bondo can be used over most metals and in most situations requiring body filler.

Many companies offer lightweight body filler, which contains tiny pieces of polystyrene. The

An alternative to chemical stripping is a new process called plastic blasting. This process uses small bits of thermo-set plastic sprayed at 40psi or less. The plastic media and lower pressure mean that paint can be safely removed from sheet metal without the damaging effects common to sandblasting. Dennis Norgaard demonstrates the process at Strip Rite in Fridley, Minnesota.

The first step is to strip off that old paint and sand down the whole tank with some 80-grit sandpaper.

47

Dennis stripped only half the tank to dramatize the effects of the process. How long it takes and how much it costs depends on the part size and how many layers of paint need to be removed. The Dry Stripping Facilities Network can put you in contact with a plastic stripping shop in your area (see Sources at the end of the book).

Gordy Larson and I outlined the ridges and valleys that make up this dent. The dent is V-locked. Undoing the damage means releasing the stress locked up in those ridges.

Gordy (known locally as the Bondo Wizard) released the stress by working on the upper ridge with a body hammer. We patiently worked the metal down, always check- *ing the progress with the hand and then adding a few more blows.*

small particles make the lightweight fillers easier to sand and work. Some customizers like to use this material to mold the frames, as the easy sanding properties are appreciated where there is much intricate hand sanding.

The third type of bondo is known as stain free. Jim McGill from PPG explained what the stain-free label means: "Sometimes, when you apply a light color or a light pearl over filler, especially if you used too much hardener in the filler, a stain develops under the paint that can be seen through the paint. We just had someone paint a beautiful 1961 Thunderbird with a white pearl paint job. After the car had been out in the sun, you could see a dark stain under the paint anywhere that the paint was sprayed over body filler. What actually happens is a reaction between the paint and the peroxides in the hardener used with the body filler. The sunlight sets off the reaction or acts as kind of a catalyst, and once the stain is there it never goes away.

"Anytime you intend to use a light pastel or pearl paint," McGill continued, "use stain-free filler. The only other way to avoid the stain is to apply two coats of black (not primer black) before applying the final paint to act as an absorber coat. The black absorbs any peroxides and acts as an ab-

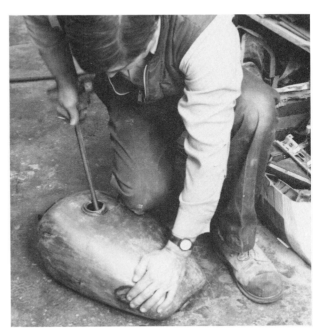

To properly unlock the dent, work up the center valley as much as possible. This is easier with an automobile fender than it is with a gas tank. Gordy was able to relieve some of the stress in the center ridge, but not as much as he wanted.

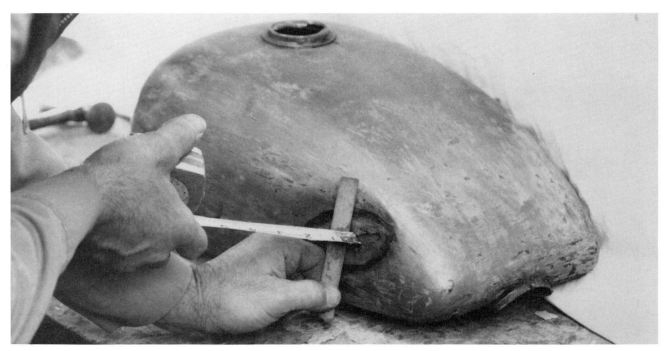

It's best to keep bondo thickness to a maximum of 1/4in—we were able to get the dent down to 3/16in.

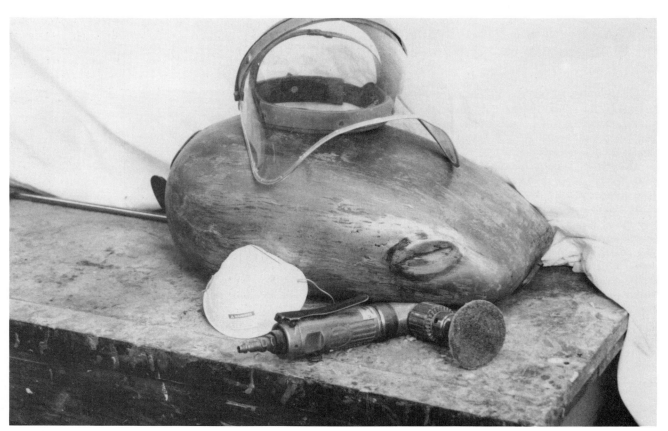

In order to ensure that the bondo will stick, you need some deep scratches—supplied by 36-grit sandpaper in this case. You can use any small air or electric drill for this; you do not need to buy a fancy grinder just to do a few motorcycle parts.

sorber between the paint and the filler. A regular sealer or primer-sealer isn't good enough to prevent the reaction."

Do's and Don'ts of Bondo Use

Everywhere you look, controversy rears its ugly head. In this case, the controversy is serious and concerns the application of body filler—should it be put over bare or primered steel? Since the days when body men (they were all men in those days) put aside their lead-working paddles and files and took up the plastic filler, bondo has been successfully applied over bare steel. Now, thirty-some years after the conversion from lead to plastic, at least one manufacturer recommends that the bondo be spread over properly prepared steel (more later) that has been painted with its two-part primer.

Before jumping into the middle of this mix-up, let's back up and talk about what constitutes a properly prepared piece of steel. Body filler bonds to the steel in two ways: mechanically and chemically. The mechanical link requires some surface roughness so the bondo can grip the metal. Most manufacturers and most of the people applying bondo day-in and day-out recommend that the steel be cleaned bare and then sanded with a 36-grit grinding pad. The deep scratches left from the 36-grit pad aid the mechanical part of the bond between filler and steel.

Until recently, everyone agreed that the chemical part of the bond worked best when the filler was applied over bare steel. Now PPG, a major paint and filler manufacturer, recommends otherwise. Jim McGill explained that you still need to grind the metal with a 36-grit pad to provide the mechanical part of the bond, but that: "you actually get a better chemical bond between bondo and our two-part primer (like DP 40) than between bondo and bare steel."

Jon Kosmoski, owner of House of Kolor and a painter and paint manufacturer for more than thirty years, feels otherwise. "We always put the bondo on over bare steel," he said, "never over a primer—not PPG's two-part or our own EP-2 and KP-2 primer."

A survey taken in the real world of small body shops and customizing operations indicates that most bondo is still being applied over bare steel, in spite of what PPG recommends.

Back to the List of Do's and Don'ts

Always make sure it is at least 60 degrees in your shop, preferably warmer, before applying bondo. Otherwise, condensation develops between the cool steel and the hot bondo (the chemical reaction that occurs as the filler hardens creates heat). Condensation can weaken the chemical bond and start the metal rusting—further weakening the bond.

Always mix the filler and hardener according to the instructions. Attempts to speed up the hardening by adding extra hardener can cause the finished bondo to be brittle or soft. In other words, when all else fails, read and follow the directions.

Gordy Larson, known to friends as the Bondo Wizard, adds a few hints: "Mix the bondo and

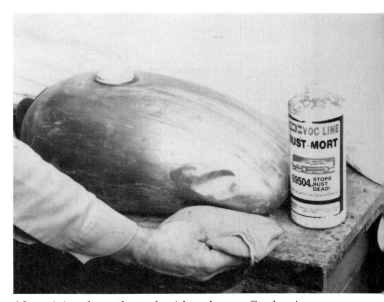

The dent itself and an area radiating 1-1/2in away from the actual dent must be scuffed with the grinder attachment. Small pads like this that take stick-on grinding discs are available from any good tool supply house.

After wiping down the tank with a cleaner, Gordy wipes it down with metal etch. This ensures the primer he sprays later will stick to the bare metal.

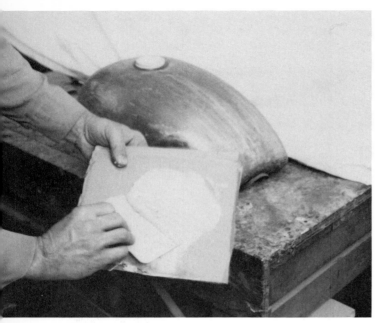

Mixing the first batch of filler and hardener. Always mix per the instructions—too little or too much hardener will affect the strength of the finished bondo.

hardener thoroughly and apply it to the steel with firm pressure to minimize air bubbles. Air bubbles are most common when it is hot out, the bubbles seem to form as the bondo cures. The air bubbles cause little pinholes that show up after the bondo is sanded. I fill these with just a little more bondo pushed into the holes with a single-edge razor blade. Spot putty works, too.

"I always put on at least two coats of bondo. The first coat I sand with 36 grit after it has set up. Then I put on a thinner second coat and sand that with 80 grit. The next step is usually primer-surfacer unless there are pinholes in the second coat of bondo. Primer won't fill pinholes, so you have to fill those with more bondo or spot putty."

Spot putties come in various types and brands. Think of these as somewhere between primer-surfacer and body filler in terms of solids content and applications. Most can be applied to imperfections too small to require the mixing of a batch of bondo. Most of these putties dry fast and sand easily. While body filler should go on over bare steel or more filler (or two-part primer in some cases), spot putties can be applied over low spots that show up after the first coat of primer has been applied.

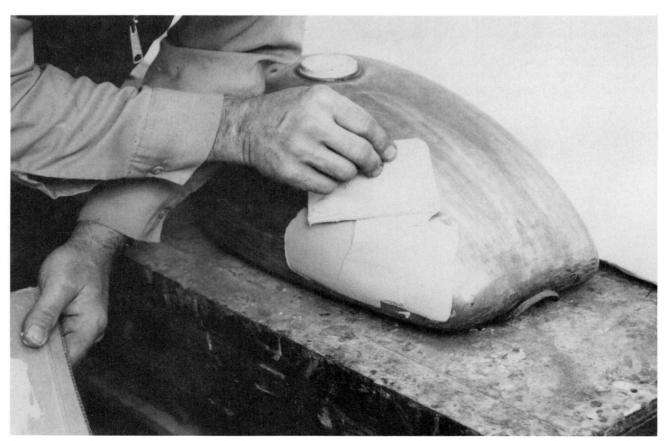

Gordy uses a plastic applicator to put the "mud" on the tank. It is important to mix the bondo thoroughly and push it on firmly to minimize air bubbles. If the dent is not too bad, two applications of bondo should be enough.

52

We start on the first coat of filler with 36-grit paper on a small sanding block. Crosshatch the bondo—sand not only vertically, but also at a 45-degree angle to the logical sanding pattern.

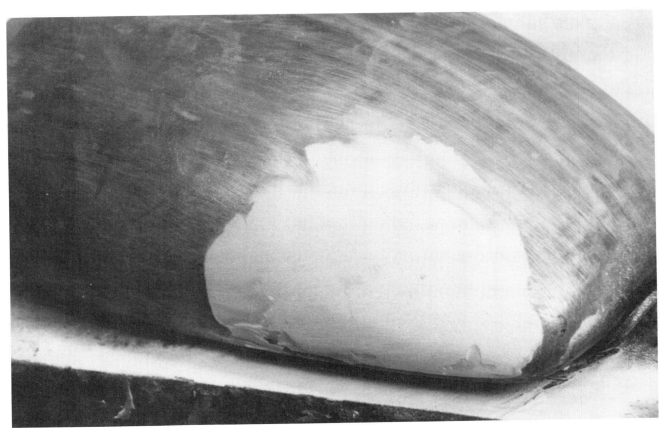

Part way through sanding the first coat, the bondo starts to take on the shape of the metal. Gordy frequently runs his hand over the bondo to gauge his progress.

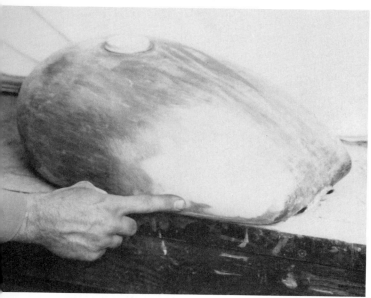

After Gordy finishes sanding the first coat, he spots a high spot in the metal. These imperfections cannot always be felt in advance; they show up after you start block sanding.

Hands-On: Removing a Dent from an Old Gas Tank

In order to better explain exactly what is involved in removing a dent from an old gas tank, Gordy Larson and I decided to do just that. The tank in question was an old swap meet refugee donated by Frog. In the lower left side was a dent roughly 2in in diameter, fairly typical of the dents that accumulate in gas tanks due to crowded parking lots, hot asphalt, sandy driveways, and Murphy's Law.

The process of restoring this old tank and removing the dent began by stripping the paint off the tank. You can find a number of stripping products on the shelf and most will do the job. We used Zip Strip and after three or four applications the paint—complete with a badly done eagle—was just a thing of the past. Some of the newer stripping products are less toxic, pose fewer disposal problems, and probably work as well as anything else.

When using a stripper, it is important to score the top surface of the paint so the stripper can penetrate faster. It is also important that the stripper be brushed on in one direction, as it contains a substance that "gels over" and prevents the rest of the stripper from drying out while it does its stuff. When you brush back and forth, the surface of the gel is broken and the stripper will dry out before it has time to penetrate the paint. Remember, too, that stripper works best when allowed to cure for the manufacturer's full recommended time. Let the stripper do its job and your job will be easier.

After the tank was stripped, Gordy examined the dent. He explained the V-lock principle discussed earlier and worked down the outer creases with a body hammer.

Next, Gordy worked a series of tools inside the tank through the gas tank opening (be careful not to mess up the sealing surface if you go this route) and worked up the crease in the center of the dent (the valley between the mountains). We tried

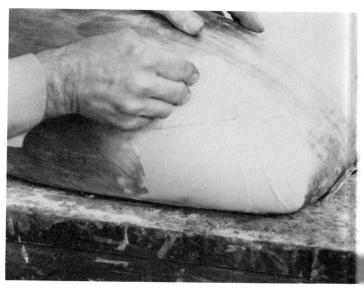

A small adjustment with the body hammer lowers the high spot to slightly less than that of the surrounding metal.

A second coat of body putty is pushed forcefully so it will fill low spots and any pinholes in the first coat of filler. It is easier and faster to achieve the right contour with two or even three coats of bondo than to try and get it right with the first coat.

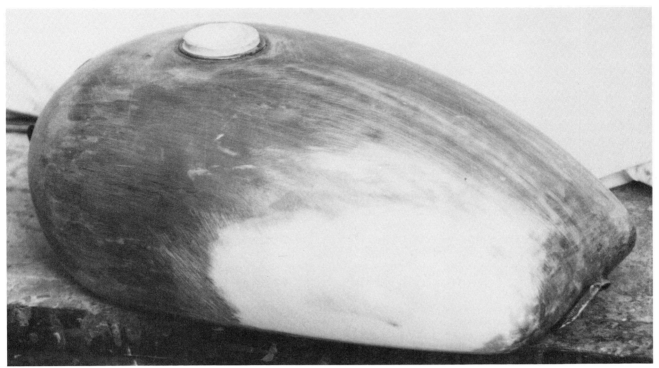

The repaired dent after sanding the second coat of bondo. Because the shape is close to the second coat, it was sanded with 80 grit on a sanding pad. Again, Gordy cross-hatched the repair and used the palm of his hand to judge his progress.

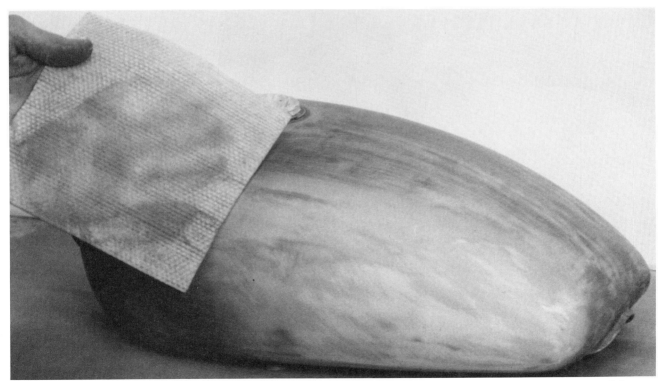

We are ready for the first coat of primer. First, we wipe down the tank with cleaner, then with a tack rag. Shown is how much material was picked up with the tack rag after the tank had already been wiped down with lacquer thinner.

everything from a large screwdriver to a body pick, which was actually made for jobs like this.

When the outer crease was knocked down level with the rest of the metal and the center crease had been worked up about 1/8in, Gordy checked the depth of the dent to make sure the bondo would not go on too thick. The dent was found to be about 3/16in thick, well within the limits for good filler application.

In order to give the filler a good surface to stick to, the area of the dent was sanded with a 36-grit pad on a small air-grinder. Of note: You do not need a big electric grinder with a 9in disc for most of this motorcycle work. A small arbor chucked into an electric or air drill is adequate for small areas like this one. The small-is-better approach is cheaper and also scores only the area you intend to apply the filler to. Remember that big grinders leave a big area of rough scratches and all those scratches have to be filled before the final paint is applied. Gordy was careful to grind only the dent and an area about 1in out from the dent.

Next, we sanded the whole tank with 80 grit to scuff off any lingering bits of paint. Although a double-action sander could have been used, a tank or two are not so big that they cannot be done by hand. Though the 80-grit surface leaves a good surface for the paint to stick to, we went ahead and treated the tank with metal etch to ensure good adhesion of the first primer coat.

Gordy mixed up a small batch of body filler and hardener, taking time to be sure the two parts were well mixed. With strong strokes, he applied the bondo in a thickness that left it with roughly the shape that would be needed to fill the dent and leave it level with the rest of the tank.

In a cool shop, fifteen minutes passed before the material was ready for sanding. Gordy warned first-time users: "In the summer, the mud sets up in about two minutes or less, so you have to be ready to mix it fast and get it on the metal before it gets too stiff."

We sanded the first coat of bondo with 36 grit paper on a small sanding pad. Again, these components are small; you do not have to buy a bunch of new sanders and grinders just to paint your motorcycle. Gordy used two tricks to help him follow the contour of the tank while sanding the body filler.

First, he ran his hand over the forward part of the tank and the damaged section, mentally comparing the contour of the two. Second, rather than always running the sanding block along the side of

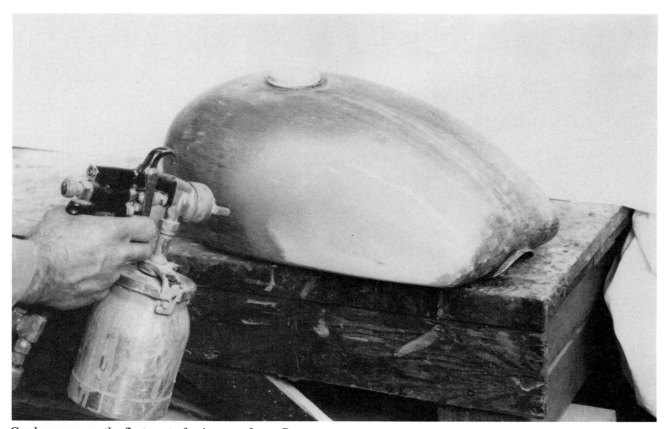

Gordy sprays on the first coat of primer-surfacer. Spray on a filler that will fill the 80-grit scratches.

the tank from front to back, he cross-hatched the repaired area with the sanding block. This process is just what it sounds like; the sanding block is run at a 45 degree angle to the natural run of the metal, and then again at 90 degrees to the first cross hatching.

After sanding the first layer for five or ten minutes, being careful to check the shape as we worked, we checked the repaired area for pinholes and high and low spots. Gordy found a high spot on the repaired area as well as some large pinholes. He also found some areas where there was not enough filler to bring the repair up to the level of the rest of the tank.

After working the metal high spot down with a hammer, we mixed and applied the second coat of bondo. Gordy pushed it hard during the application to fill the holes in the first coat of filler.

Ten minutes later, Gordy sanded the second coat of bondo with 80-grit sandpaper mounted to the same small sanding block used earlier. This coat was not as thick so we did not need such coarse paper, and the 80-grit scratches were easier to fill with primer-surfacer.

Once again, we worked with the sanding block from front to back, as well as in the cross-hatch pattern. This time, no metal high spots came through the sanding. Soon, Gordy had the repaired area smooth, with a contour that matched the rest of the tank.

We wiped down the tank with Prep Sol (a good wax and grease remover also works) to remove any lingering stripper that might be waiting in a crevice to spoil our paint job. We wiped the tank down with a tack rag to remove any lingering dust.

After two coats of primer-surfacer (the number of coats applied depends on the paint and the manufacturer's recommendations), we allowed the primer paint to dry. The next step was to block-sand the whole tank with 180-grit paper on the small sanding block. There is no need for cross-hatching now because we fill scratches with the primer-surfacer. The block sanding is important from this point on; it is a great aid to show high and low spots. If you sanded the tank with your hand, your fingers followed the contour of the tank and low spots might go undiscovered. The block scuffs all the areas except those that are low. The difference in the finish of the primer after the

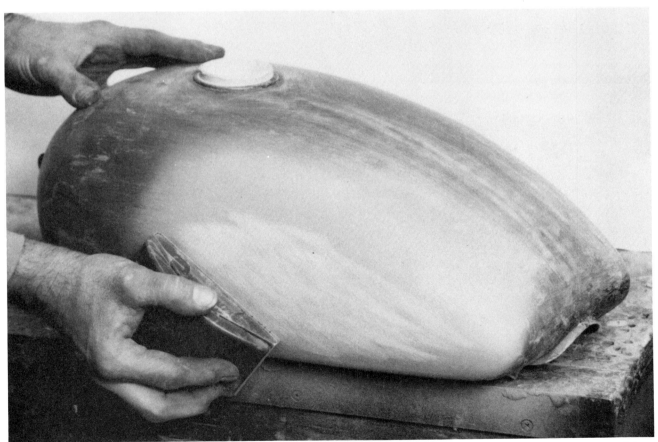

We block sand the repair with 180 grit to fill the earlier scratches, sand off any high spots, and show up any lingering low spots. Gordy sands both vertically and in a crosshatch pattern.

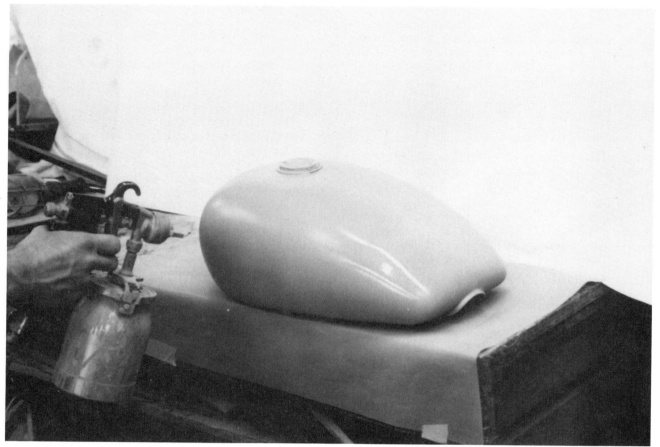

After wiping down the tank with cleaner and a tack rag, we spray it with primer-surfacer.

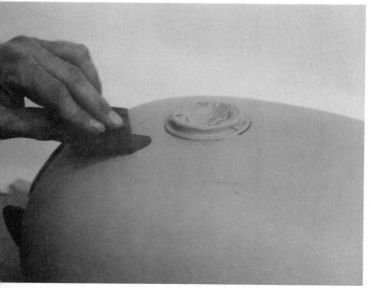

Gordy applies spot putty to a low spot that became evident after spraying the primer-surfacer. Spot putties dry quickly and can be applied to small low spots like this one.

sanding operation shows any significant high and low areas.

In order to create a truly fine paint finish, the surface must be flat, flat, flat and perfectly smooth. The way to achieve that surface is by block-sanding again and again using finer and finer sandpaper.

After our first block sanding operation, Gordy found a low spot near the filler that we were not aware of before and one low area in the part where body filler was used. A little spot putty easily filled those depressions. The putty dried quickly and Gordy went over the puttied areas with 180 grit on the sanding block. Then it was time to wipe the puttied areas down with a cleanser and apply primer-surfacer.

Now the whole tank was block sanded with 320-grit paper on the sanding block. The relatively fine paper took longer to cut the paint, but soon Gordy found some subtle low spots. He applied another coat of primer-surfacer after wiping it down with Prep Sol and then did the whole tank again with the sanding block. Finding no more spots low enough to fill, Gordy applied another coat of

Our two low spots are sanded with 180 grit on a sanding block. Two coats of spot putty may be required to get the spots level with the surrounding metal.

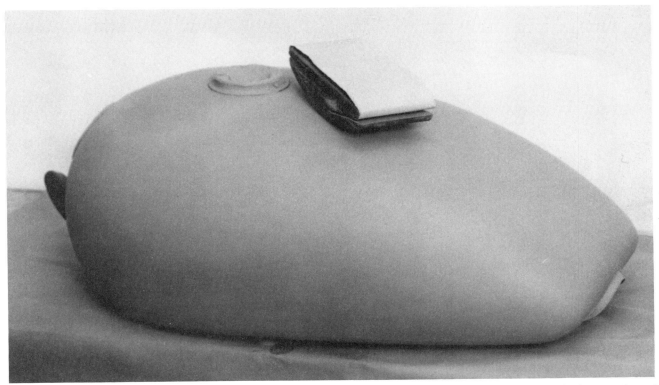

The tank is coated again with primer-surfacer and then sanded with 320 grit. During this block sanding, you may find more low spots that need spot putty or more primer-surfacer. How far you go with this routine of sanding and filling is up to you.

Gordy sprays the tank with one more coat of primer-surfacer and then block sands with 400 grit on a flexible sanding pad. The flexible pad follows the contour of the tank without allowing your fingers to put grooves in the primer.

primer-surfacer and then went over the tank one more time with a flexible pad and some 400-grit paper. We were not looking for low spots now, so we changed to a flexible pad that followed the contours of the tank. At this point we were trying to create a uniform scuffed surface—the flexible pad followed contours yet did not cut subtle grooves in the paint from our fingers.

At Last!

The tank was now finished and ready for final paint. The final steps depend on how fussy you are and the paint system you use. Though 320 is the minimal grit for the final finish, many painters use 400 or even 600 grit to ensure that the surface is really smooth. Likewise, the final coat of primer might be a primer-sealer if that is the recommendation of the final paint manufacturer.

We accomplished the removal of a small dent. In fact, the area with the dent looks exactly the same as the rest of the tank—and that was the whole idea.

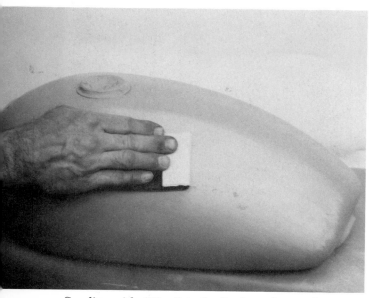

Sanding with 400 grit is the final repair step. Some people will go farther, to 500 or 600 grit for example, but essentially the tank is ready for sealer and finish paint.

Chapter 5

Painting and Molding the Frame

More Work, But Well Worth It

One of the major decisions in planning a motorcycle paint job is whether or not to paint the frame. As mentioned earlier, by painting the frame you open up new possibilities in terms of colors and paint schemes. When you decide to paint the frame, you also have the option of molding the frame. Molding is smoothing out those rough factory welds and the fabricated additions at

Painting the Frame

If you settle for a plain, one-color paint job for your frame, the whole job is simple. You might wonder whether it is better to sand the frame or to strip it down to bare metal. Late-model Harleys have powder coated frames, a durable material. You could probably sand down that paint and spray over the powder coating. Yet there are ad-

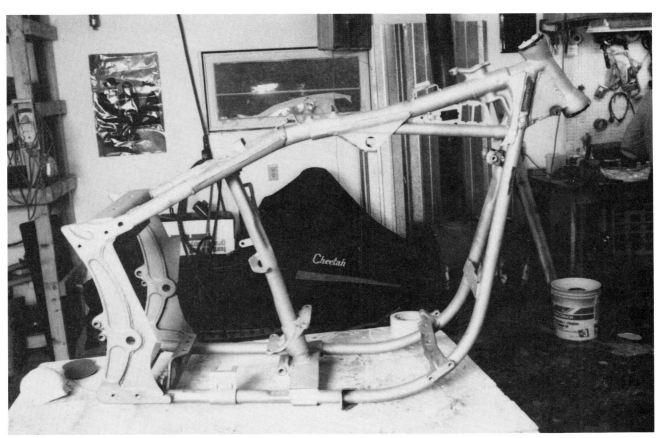

The before picture: a Softail frame ready for molding. All the rough factory welds and the fabricated additions at the back of the frame will be smoothed and made seamless.

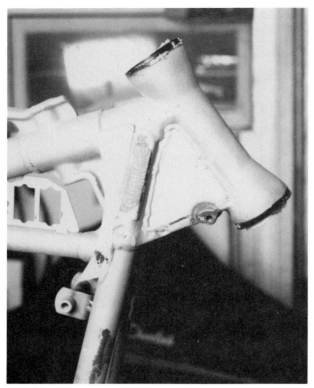

The neck area. The concave triangle between the tubes and the neck will be filled in completely with bondo.

vantages to stripping it down to bare metal. As the infamous Mallard Teal said: "I like to strip the frame bare. If you sand it, then you've got to sand every little nook and cranny, you've got to be sure you get all the grease and dirt out of the little crevices. It seems easier to me to just strip off all the paint, that way I know there isn't any crud trapped someplace that I didn't get clean or an area that didn't get sanded."

Once you have the frame down to bare metal, treat the metal with a metal-etching product (or a self-etching primer) followed by primer and then primer-surfacer. You can spray some of the two-part primers directly over treated bare metal, and some are sandable, eliminating the need for a separate primer and primer-surfacer coat. For a nice pre-paint surface, use a primer-surfacer sanded with fine paper, at least 320 grit and maybe finer. Before the finish paint, apply a primer-sealer. The primer-sealer provides good color hold out, meaning the final coats will look nice and bright just like the chips on the paint card.

Note: Each manufacturer's primer products are a little different. Some of the two-part primers are listed as "easily sandable" and some are not, so read all the labels and ask the paint jobber for help. As stated earlier, get the technical information sheets for each paint product you use. These sheets contain a wealth of information regarding

Greg Smith starts the job by grinding down the areas that will be molded. When grinding on factory welds, it is important that only a small amount of metal be removed—taking too much would weaken the joint.

62

mixing, use, and compatibility of the various paints.

When it comes to choosing a paint for the frame of your Harley, use a catalyzed urethane. These paints are durable, providing good protection from rock chips, sand abrasion, and oil and gas spills. The only more durable coating would be powder coating, a good option if you want the ultimate in durability.

If you do not like using the catalyzed products in your home garage because of their toxicity, you can always have the frame painted by a commercial painter and paint the rest of the bike at home with lacquer or enamel.

Molding the Frame

Molding is a matter of smoothing out all those rough factory welds. The operation starts by stripping the paint off the frame. At the very least, strip the paint from the joint areas where you will apply the filler.

The first part of the molding operation involves grinding down the welds. Greg Smith (brother to motorcycle builder Donnie Smith, seen in some of the accompanying photos) explains: "People shouldn't get too carried away when they grind on the weld or they can really weaken the welded joint. All you want to do is knock the top off the weld and then grind the area around the weld so the plastic filler will stick." The grinding should be done with a 24- or a 36-grit grinding pad on a

small grinder. Using a coarse grinding pad will leave some deep scratches in the metal, giving the filler something to hold onto.

After mixing a small batch of bondo per the instructions on the can (you can speed up the hardening by adding additional hardener but it tends to make the bondo more brittle), apply the mixture by hand. Use small trowels and plastic paddles in some areas, but in others gob it on your finger and work it around the frame tubing. Most paint supply stores have plastic filler in various weights. Greg Smith recommends using the lightweight bondo, which contains chips of polystyrene, because it is more flexible and sands more easily.

As you apply the mud, think of yourself as an artist or sculptor, creating graceful curves where rough corners existed before. Make gradual curves without letting the total bondo thickness go much past 1/2in. Yes, this is thicker than the manufacturers recommend, but there just is not anything you can do to avoid this little problem. The filler needs to be put on in a series of layers, each one

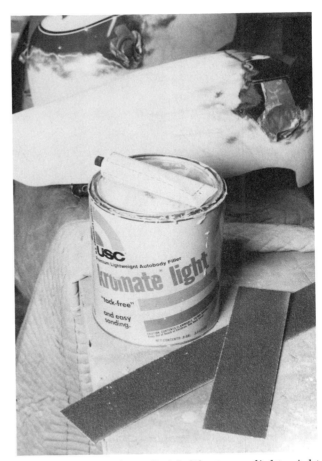

Pete Wilson and Greg Smith like to use lightweight bondo. Not to be confused with light beer, this filler contains small particles of plastic making it flexible and easy to sand and shape.

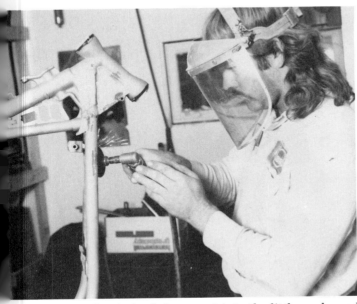

A small grinder helps to get into the little nooks and crannies. Thirty-six-grit pads are used so the grinding marks will be deep and the bondo will have something to hold onto. A small electric drill equipped with a sanding disc could be used here—you do not have to buy expensive air-powered grinders.

Greg uses a variety of grinders to ease the work load. In a home shop, an electric drill equipped with a grinding/sanding pad attachment could be used also.

not more than 3/16in thick. After the first coat has set up, smooth it with 36-grit sandpaper. In some areas, you can create nice curves with only two or three layers of mud, though others will need four or more layers before they look good.

In an area where you need to create a curve with a certain radius, take the advice of Jim McGill, PPG paint rep: "I find a wooden dowel with the right diameter and get some self-adhering sandpaper. I stick the sandpaper to the dowel and use that to give me exactly the curve I want. You can get dowels of almost any diameter at the lumberyard; you can even put a handle on the dowel if you want to get fancy."

After you have worked each area into a good-looking shape, put on a layer of glaze or putty. Most of these are two-part products, similar to the bondo but much thinner, designed to help fill the 36-grit scratches. When the glaze coat has dried, sand it with 80-grit paper, followed by a spray application of a good primer-surfacer. Greg Smith used K 200 two-part primer-surfacer from PPG, sprayed over the glaze. He sanded the first coat of primer-surfacer with 180 grit followed by another coat of primer-surfacer, sanded with 600 grit. How fine you go on the final sanding is a matter of per-

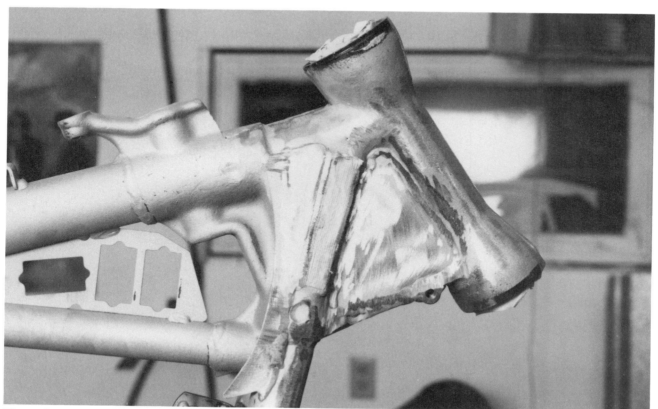

The neck area after it has been worked over with a 36-grit grinding pad. Greg was careful to leave the number ID pad intact so the bike can be easily identified.

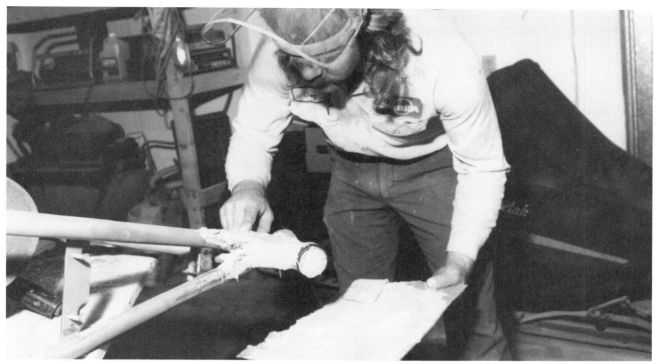

Greg uses a high-tech tool—his fingers—to apply and shape the filler material. He suggests that the total thick- *ness of the filler should not go much past 3/8in, and should be put on in two or three layers.*

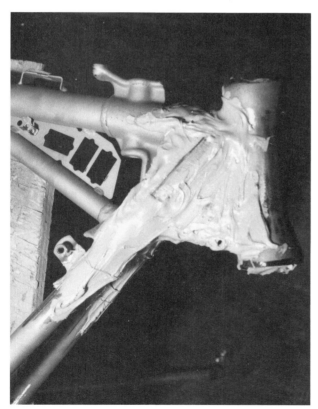

The neck after the first application of filler. Note again that the number ID pad has been left intact.

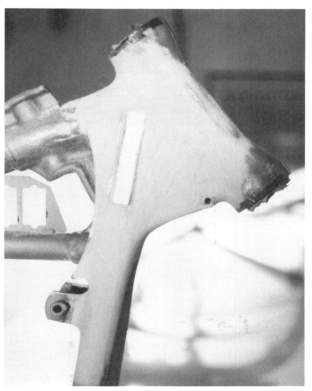

After the first coat of bondo has been sanded down with 36-grit grinding pads and sandpaper, little of the factory welds can be seen.

sonal opinion. Some shops only go to 320 grit while others insist on 600 or even 800 grit.

Following the final sanding, apply one last coat of primer-sealer (some two-part primers can be used as sealers). This coat is usually not sanded. Finally, apply the final topcoat of paint.

In Conclusion

Painting the frame is a dirty job, but somebody has to do it. Although painting or molding the frame is tons of work, it adds a great deal to the total look of the bike. Like any other painting operation, the key is careful preparation, quality materials, and patience.

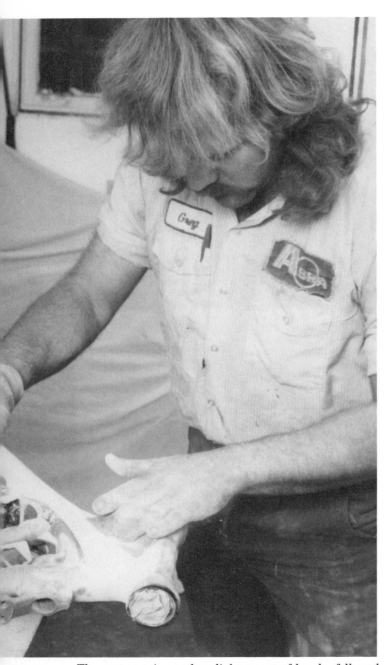

The next step is another, lighter coat of bondo, followed by more sanding and shaping. Here, Greg sands the second coat of bondo with 80-grit paper. Once he has the right shape in bondo, he will apply one or two coats of glaze (a lighter filler) working gradually to a 180-grit paper.

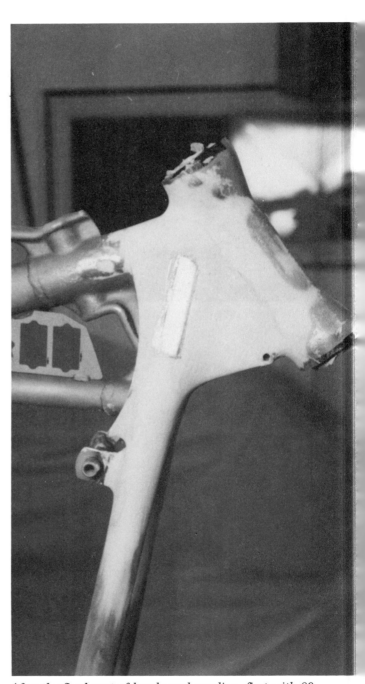

After the final coat of bondo and sanding, first with 80 and then 180 paper, the area between the neck and the tubes has a smooth contour and requires only more finishing with glaze before the primer-surfacer.

Pete Wilson works by hand, filling the welds at the back of the frame.

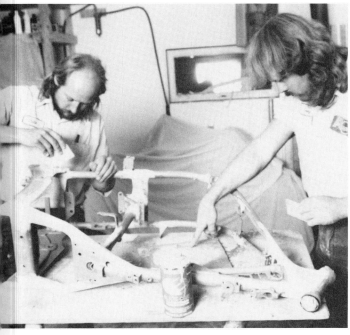

The first glaze coat is applied to fill the scratches in the plastic filler. Note that Pete uses a flexible pad while Greg works with his finger.

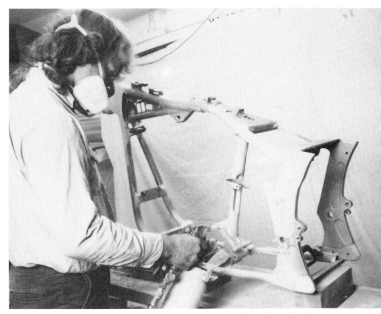

After the bondo came the glaze and after the glaze had been sanded, Greg sprayed on a coat of K 200 primer-surfacer. After he and Pete have sanded the K 200 and sprayed the frame with a primer sealer it will ready to paint.

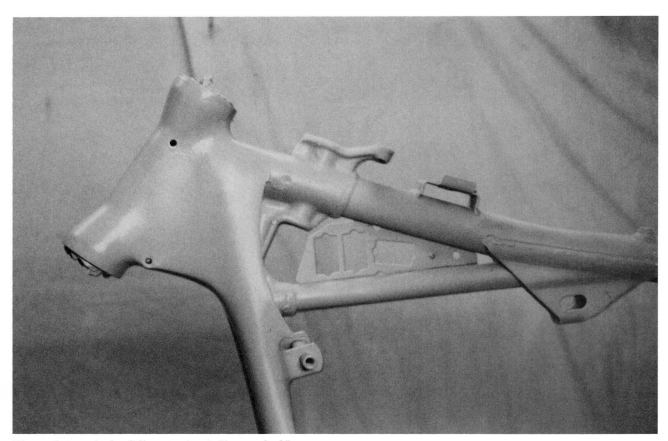

The neck area looks different now. A "factory look" was achieved by applying the filler so that the curves look natural and graceful.

Chapter 6

Engine Painting

It Does Not Have to be Polished

If you look at bikes built by professional builders like Donnie Smith, Dave Perewitz, and a few others, you soon see that many of them carry engines with painted—rather than polished—engine cases and cylinders. Dave Perewitz often paints the cases black and the cylinders in black wrinkle paint. The polished or stainless bolt heads used to hold these engines together contrast nicely with the black paint. Black also goes well with any color combination and gives the engine a nice all-business look.

Alternatively, you can use the engine color to contrast or complement the colors used on the rest of the bike. The ultra Fat Boy that Donnie Smith built for Drag Specialties carries an engine painted hot blue. The hot blue contrasts with the hot pink and deep rose used on the rest of the bike. To give the bike a well-integrated look, the hot blue was also used on parts of the frame and air dam.

The color you choose is up to you. Painting the engine adds considerable work to the project, but it also opens up a range of possibilities as far as your color scheme is concerned. When you plan your paint project, determine first if the engine is going to come out of the frame. If so, you have one more thing to think about as you determine the colors for your new ride.

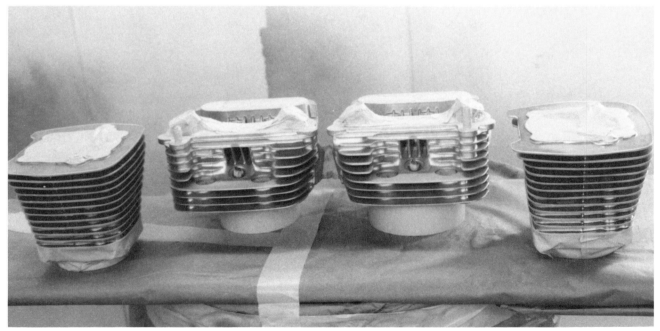

These barrels and heads have been bead blasted then wiped down with Prep Sol to get them truly clean (although you could settle for a good cleaning with solvent followed by Prep Sol or lacquer thinner). The bead blasting gives the paint a somewhat coarse surface on which to stick.

Mallard sprays on the DP 50, a catalyzed primer. It is important to spray the parts from a number of angles and invert them so all the surfaces between the fins get covered.

The edges of the fins have been polished. The polished area is taped off before any painting starts.

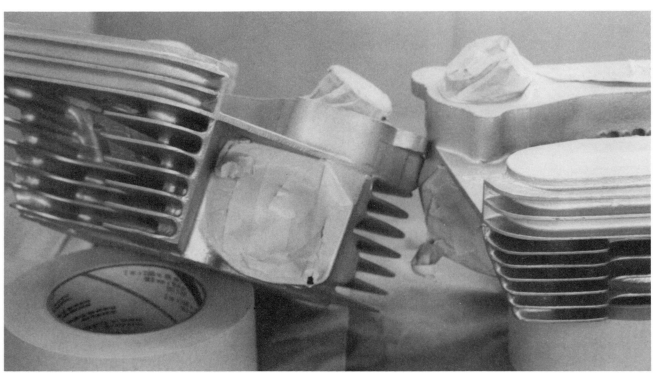

These cylinder heads are ready to paint. Painting heads presents something of a quandary—although they look good overall, there is always some discoloration at the exhaust port due to the extreme temperatures. Heads are also hard to mask because of the studs and unusual shapes. Masking these parts is just as much work as painting them.

It is difficult to wipe down these parts with a cleaner or tack rag. About all you can do for a final cleaning before painting is blow them off with compressed air.

Preparation

Like any painting operation, preparation is the most important part of painting your engine. Cleanliness is the first step. A perfect preparation sequence includes disassembly of the engine, care-

ful cleaning of all components, and bead blasting before the actual painting begins.

In the real world, you may not want to completely disassemble a perfectly good engine. Harley engines can and have been successfully painted

Here, all the parts have had a two-part catalyzed primer applied, which is used for its tenacious bonding and great durability. During painting the cylinders were in- *verted once and paint sprayed from a number of different angles.*

Mallard puts on the first of two base coats, using DBU base coat colors from PPG. He works over the barrels *again and again, approaching from different angles, to get paint between all those fins.*

without a complete disassembly and without bead blasting the cases and components. The key again is cleanliness. Jerry Scherer, who has painted many Harleys, likes to start the cleaning with lacquer thinner followed by Acryli-Clean (a Prep Sol type of cleaning solvent that leaves no film behind). After the components are clean, clean, clean, Jerry sprays on DP 50 primer (a light gray catalyzed primer from PPG), topcoated with catalyzed urethane, and followed by a urethane clear coat.

Light Aqua heads and violet barrels tinted to match the colors used on the rest of the bike.

If the engine is very dirty, use strong dish soap and hot water (a great grease cutting combination) as the first step in the cleaning process followed by lacquer thinner and Prep Sol. It is important to remove all the grease and any old paint. It is equally important that the final cleaning product leaves no film on the metal.

Painting the Engine

Primer choices for the engine should be narrowed down to a good catalyzed primer because these paints adhere to the aluminum better than a simple lacquer primer. Most painters do not use a metal etch before applying the primer, though you might want to check with your paint supplier for a recommendation.

Jon Kosmoski likes to use a zinc-chromate type of two-part primer because it adheres so well to the aluminum. He recommends his own EP 2 or KP 2, or DuPont's Corlar.

Any good finish paint can be applied to your engine cases including, of course, a durable catalyzed urethane. Most professional painters prefer the catalyzed urethane for engines and engine components because it resists heat, rock chips, and stains from gas and oil better than anything else except powder coating.

Simplified engine painting can be accomplished through the use of specialized paints. Harley-Davidson sells black wrinkle paint that can be applied to your engine without the use of primer. Available in spray cans or by the quart, the painter sprays it directly on the aluminum without any primer. The other option is the Very High Temperature (VHT) paint, which is designed to be used on engines and engine components. VHT paint is sold in auto parts stores. Although the VHT paint might not have the durability of a good urethane paint, it has a large convenience factor of being available in spray can form working in its favor.

A Two-Tone V-Twin for a Two-Tone Harley

In Chapter 8, Mallard Teal of St. Paul, Minnesota, paints his own Harley FXR. He chose lavender and Light Aqua colors, both modified by the tinted clear sprayed on top of the color coats.

Mallard decided that what was good for the bike was equally good for the engine. The engine was pulled apart so Mallard could paint the barrels and heads. He chose a urethane from PPG, covered in a tinted clear (think of it as a light candy coat) followed by clear. There was a small problem with painting heads, however. "The paint usually discolors around the exhaust port from the heat," Mallard explained, "there isn't much you can do about it."

Before Mallard started painting, he had the heads and barrels bead blasted and the edges of the fins on the barrels polished. When the heads and barrels came back to his shop, the polished fins were taped off with thin masking tape. (You could paint the barrels and polish the fin edges after painting, but there would be much polishing compound left on the barrels to be cleaned off.)

Both the heads and barrels were primered in DP 50, a catalyzed primer from PPG. Mallard applied one good coat of primer, being careful to spray from two or three angles and with the parts in at least two positions so primer would find its way to all the nooks and crannies.

After the primer dried, Mallard started with the colors. Both the Purple Velvet and Light Aqua are DBU universal base coat colors from PPG, designed to be covered with a clear coat. Both were sprayed in two coats—again the parts were inverted once during each painting operation, and Mallard repeatedly changed the gun's angle to get paint into the areas between the fins.

After the DBU base coats had flashed, Mallard topcoated them with a tinted clear and a final coat of clear. Mallard went to this extreme to be sure

Freshly painted barrels, stripped of their masking tape. Like any other custom painting project, it is important to pull the tape off as soon as possible.

the engine parts would match the colors on the sheet metal. Most people would simply paint the parts with base coat and cover them with one or two coats of clear.

The final step was to pull the tape off the edges of the fins as soon as possible and wait for the paint to dry. When it was all over, Mallard had some bright and colorful barrels and heads: aqua and violet—not your standard Harley engine colors.

Wrap-Up

Painting an engine is not especially difficult. It usually requires that the motor come out of the frame, and it adds an additional series of operations to your paint job. But it also adds a new dimension to the project. Even if all you do is paint it black, the engine will take on a new look. And if you use your imagination, you can make the engine an essential part of a colorful motorcycle.

Elaborate engine paint jobs like this one take much work, but of course Mallard thinks it is worthwhile. This type of paint job cannot be done without complete disassembly.

Chapter 7

A Simple Two-tone Candy Paint Job

From Start to Finish

When it comes to learning a new skill, it is hard to beat the hands-on approach. Far be it from me to minimize the value of book learning, but in the end it is nice to learn a skill directly from someone who does it day after day. In order to give readers a hands-on feel to this business of learning how to paint a motorcycle, this chapter follows a simple two-tone candy paint job from start to finish.

Though some of the steps will be repetitious with procedures covered in Chapter 8, repeating these steps is the only way to show readers what happens in the real world. Astute readers will notice that sometimes there are differences between the methods recommended by the paint manufacturers and those followed in the paint shops. These can only be called legitimate differences of opinion

The before picture. The large Sportster tank's paint has blistered around the gas cap, a chronic problem for motorcycles. Paint on the tank also did not match the facto- *ry paint on the fenders so the decision was made to give the bike a complete paint job.*

and another example that there are at least two ways to do almost anything.

A Two-Tone Candy Job for a Sportster

The Sportster seen here is a good example of a simple candy paint job. Although the bike is only three years old, the paint on the king-sized tank was peeling at the gas opening—a common problem with motorcycle paint jobs. As long as the tank had to be painted, it seemed best to paint the whole bike. The original color was a deep blue/purple with metallic. The new colors were chosen to stay on the blue end of the color spectrum.

The paint job started by chemically stripping off the old paint. Though we probably could have stripped the tank and sanded the fenders, the paint on the fenders was starting to crack and seemed thick in places. By stripping off all the paint, we eliminated the risk of putting paint on too heavy, causing cracking later, or of having a reaction between the new paint and the old paint underneath. (A good alternative to chemical stripping is a new plastic-blasting process (see illustrations). Don't take your sheet metal to a commercial sand-

blaster, as sandblasting creates enough heat to warp panels.)

First, we took a razor blade and scribed the paint surface. These heavy scratches made it possible for the paint stripper to penetrate into the paint faster and shortened the time needed for the stripping operation. The stripper we used is Klean Strip Aircraft Remover.

It took three applications of the stripper to get all the paint off the tank and fenders. The key is in using a scribe or razor blade to break the surface of the paint and then having enough patience to let the stripper do its job. After three applications, we had nearly all the paint off the parts and finished up any small areas with a piece of sandpaper.

Before spraying the parts with primer, the tank and fenders were sanded down with a double-action sander with a 180-grit pad. This removed any lingering paint and left a lightly scuffed surface for the primer to stick to.

If any residual stripper was left on the parts, it would cause a reaction with the new paint. After all the paint was removed from the surfaces we

Because it was not known what type of paint was used on the tank and the paint looked thick on the fenders, we decided to strip off all the paint. When in doubt, strip. Many good strippers are available, and some of the new
materials are much less toxic and easier to use than older products. Brush on stripper with an old paint brush always moving in one direction. Wear gloves and work in a well ventilated area.

Use a putty knife to peel off paint. The tank was scored with a razor blade before the stripper was applied so that the chemicals could quickly work down under the paint surface. Three applications were needed to remove all the paint.

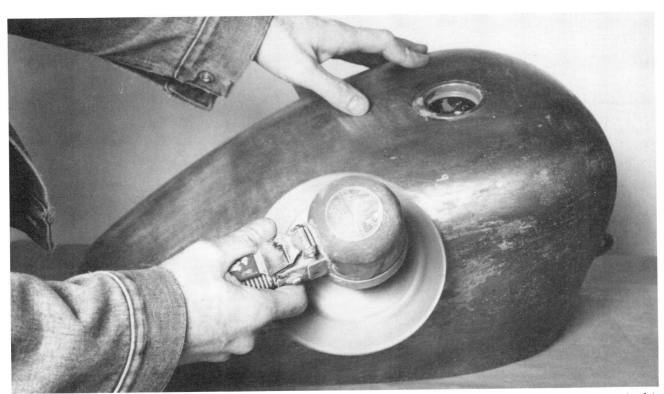

We used a double-action sander with a 180-grit paper to remove any lingering paint. This operation could have been done by hand. In fact, hand work was required in spots where the sanding pad would not go.

After sanding, the tank got a good cleaning with lacquer thinner to remove any lingering stripper. There were no low spots that needed filler so the tank is nearly ready for the first coat of primer.

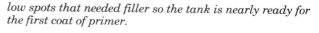

Before applying primer, we decided to wipe down the tank with a metal etch. Think of it as a primer for the primer; metal etch removes any light surface rust and ensures that the first coat of paint will adhere to the bare steel.

would paint, the parts were rinsed off with water and wiped down with lacquer thinner. The wipe down included the bottom side of the tank and fenders. Mallard explained that it is important to get rid of any lingering stripper. "If there's any stripper left on those parts," he explained, "it will cause a failure of the new paint job—you will have to paint everything over again."

The final preparation step before spraying primer was to wipe down the parts with Kwik Prep, a metal conditioner or metal etch from DuPont. Similar products are made by a variety of companies. The Kwik Prep was wiped over the surfaces with a clean rag. Most of these products improve adhesion between the bare metal and the first primer coat as well as remove any minor rust or oxidation. A final note on metal-etch products: some of these are meant to be diluted with water, some are wiped off after being applied, while others are left on to dry—be sure to follow the product's directions.

Our next step was to spray all the parts with their first coat of primer. Mallard used DP 50 from PPG, a two-part primer noted for good adhesion and corrosion resistance. DP 50 is not a primer-surfacer, so after the first primer coat was dry, we

Here, the tank has received a coat of DP 50—a catalyzed primer from PPG. Catalyzed (or two-part) primers are a good idea on motorcycle tanks as they help prevent spilled gas from seeping under the topcoat and spoiling the paint job.

The next step is two coats of this K 36 primer-surfacer. Even though the metal looks smooth and flat, it isn't. This fast-build material allows us to fill any small irregularities and create a truly flat surface for the final paint.

79

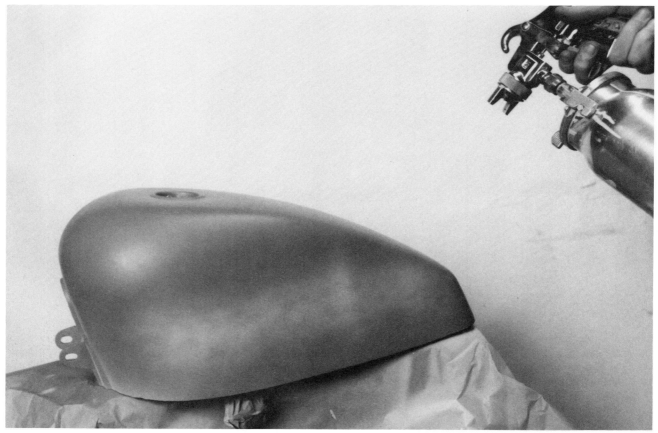

The K 36 is sprayed on in two coats, one light and one heavy, to provide enough material to fill small low spots

or scratches. This is a two-part primer surfacer that adheres well to the primer beneath it and sands easily.

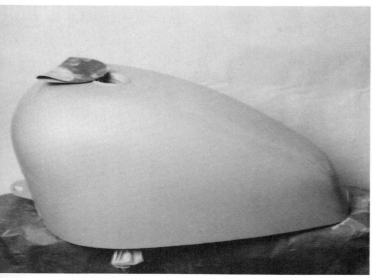

How fine a sandpaper you use before applying final paint is a matter of preference—we used 400-grit paper to sand the K 36 perfectly flat. Although it is hard to see, the K 36 takes on a sheen as it is sanded. What we really did was polish the K 36 primer-surfacer, creating a flat surface and eliminating any small high or low spots.

sprayed the tank and fenders with Prima. This is a two-part primer-surfacer from PPG, known by part number K 36 and hardener K 201. This is a high-solids, fast-drying, and easy-sanding primer-surfacer. The color is a light gray (it can be tinted) and it sands easily, making it easy to block sand the tank and fenders.

Like all the modern materials, especially the two-part primers and paints, Prima must be mixed and used according to the directions. We allowed the mixed Prima to incubate for thirty minutes in the pot before spraying. Mallard sprayed on one light coat, which was allowed to dry for fifteen minutes, before applying a second, heavy coat.

Because the tank and fenders were in good condition with no dents or dings, the Prima was all the preparation needed to create a flat and smooth surface. With no dents, we did not need to use bondo or spot putty to fill irregularities—the primer-surfacer would be adequate to fill any sanding scratches.

After allowing the primer-surfacer to dry overnight, it was time for sanding and more sanding. We used 400-grit paper and lots of water to sand the Prima. This is a case where first-time

After more than two hours of sanding on the tank and fenders they are ready for paint. During the sanding, run your hand over the surface frequently so you can feel the difference as the surface becomes flatter and smoother.

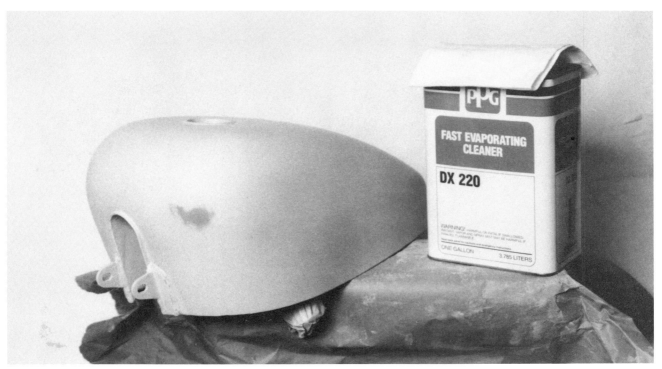

We cleaned the tank with DX 220 cleaner after the sanding was finished. You need a cleaner that leaves no residue behind after evaporation.

Mallard uses a tack rag just before applying the next coat of paint.

painters will have to educate their hand. What at first feels like a smooth surface to a novice is not good enough. In effect, the continual sanding is actually polishing the Prima until, eventually, it takes on a sheen. By running your hand over the surface after plenty of sanding, you will learn what "smooth" really feels like.

The key to a truly good-looking paint job is a flat surface; you can only achieve that perfectly flat surface after sanding with fine paper over a good primer-surfacer. "Keep sanding until you are really sure it is a good surface," Mallard advised. "If you sand through in a few places, it won't hurt because you are going to put on a final layer of DP 50 before you put on final paint anyway. And if you sand through too many places you can just spray on another coat of the primer-surfacer."

When the surface finally met Mallard's standards, we went over the parts with a tack rag and sprayed on another coat of DP 50. In this case, the DP 50 is used as a primer-sealer (in some cases you might want to put on a product sold specifically as a sealer). This primer-sealer would prevent the topcoats from sinking into the layers underneath and dulling the final colors.

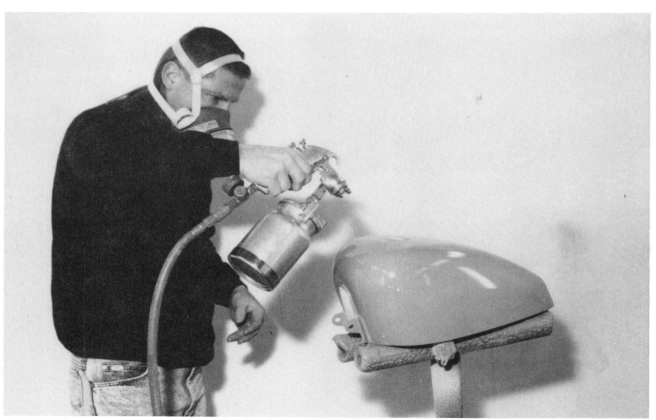

Another coat of DP 50 two-part primer is sprayed on before spraying on the finish paint. In this case, we use the DP 50 as a sealer coat—be sure you use an appropriate primer-sealer before applying the topcoats. This coat of DP 50 was not sanded before the next coat of paint was applied.

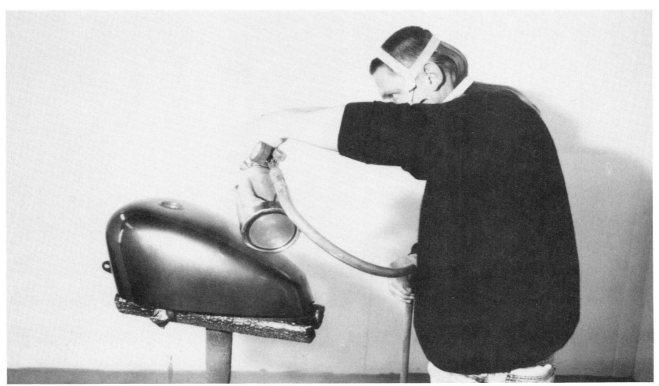

Mallard applies the first base coat for this base coat/candy coat paint job. We had to wait at least one hour after applying the DP 50 before applying the base coats. Waiting times for any particular painting system must be closely followed.

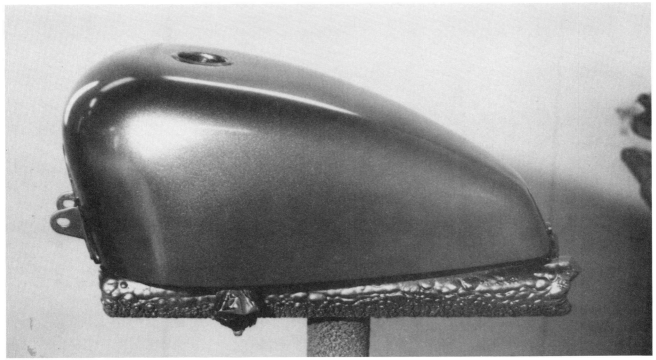

This base coat is two coats of Pace Car Blue, a blue metallic base coat from the PPG Radiance II line of paints. Mallard waited fifteen minutes between the two coats.

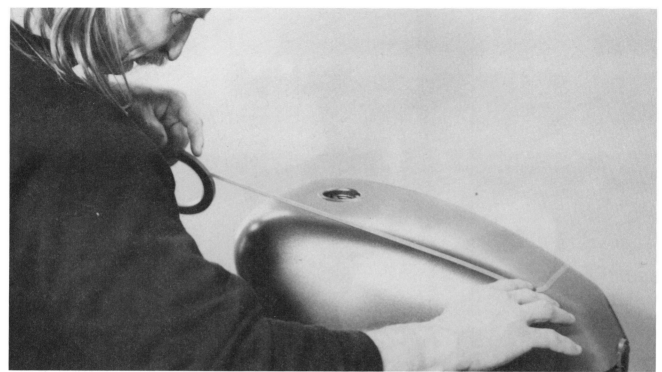

After waiting one hour, the Pace Car Blue was dry enough to apply tape and create the simple two-tone pattern of Mallard's choice. The idea is a subtle two-tone job created by using two different base coats under the same candy topcoat. Mallard uses 3M plastic tape for tape-outs such as this one and does his designing on the tank or fender.

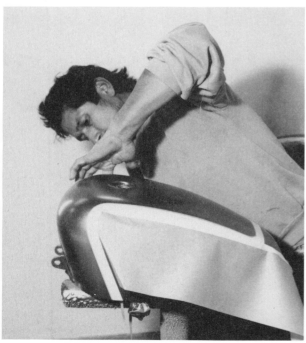

Masking paper and 3/4in tape are used to mask off the design on the tank and fenders. Joe Damora makes sure the tape is well stuck to the tank so no paint will creep under the tape's edge.

The final primer-sealer coat was not sanded. After drying overnight, it was time to apply the base coats for our base coat/candy coat paint job. The design, which Mallard Teal conceived, is a simple and conservative one. Mallard's simple two-tone paint job would consist of a Cobalt Blue candy top coat sprayed over two different base coats to give a subtle two-tone effect. The two base coats are Pace Car Blue and Sterling Silver. All the paints used are from the PPG Radiance II line and all are urethanes (these same color combinations are also available in acrylic lacquer).

Mallard started the base coat application with Pace Car Blue. This is a high-solids paint, and only two medium coats, with fifteen minutes tack time between coats, were required to give the desired color. One hour after the second coat, the paint was dry enough to tape (this "dry enough to tape" time will depend on the individual paint). As a note, many of these base coats have a flat finish and get their gloss from the candy or clear coat.

First-time painters will probably want to draw out their design on paper, before transferring it to the metal. Mallard and many experienced custom painters go directly from mind to metal. They use plastic tape from 3M to tape-out the design, working strictly by hand (plastic tape can be bent into more complex shapes than conventional masking

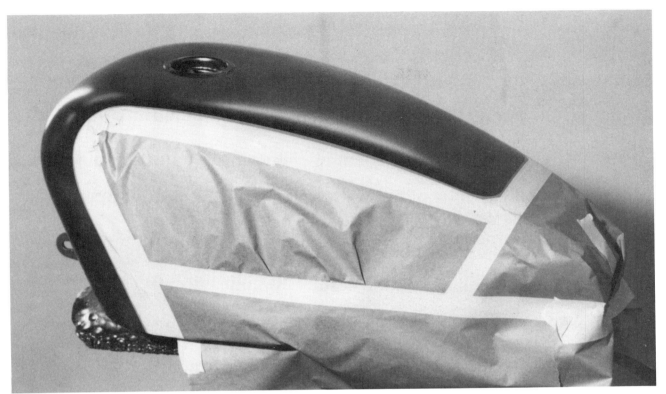

Ready for the next step. Newspaper can be used in place of masking paper. Just don't be cheap with the tape, and be sure to take your time and do a neat job.

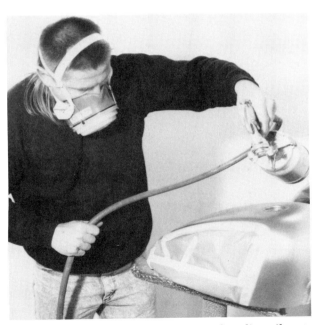

Mallard applies the second base coat of sterling silver to the tank's center, fifteen minutes after the first. Between-coat-times are dependant on the particular paint and the conditions in your shop. Note that the gun is kept at a 90-degree angle to the surface and that Mallard holds the air hose with his other hand so it cannot touch the paint job.

tape). After taping out the design, the rest of the area where we did not want any of the second base color was taped over with regular masking tape.

Next, two medium coats of Sterling Silver were applied to the tank and fenders. The tape

Our tank after we removed the tape and paper. We removed the tape as soon as possible to avoid any chance that it would dry and tear the final coats of paint as it was removed.

85

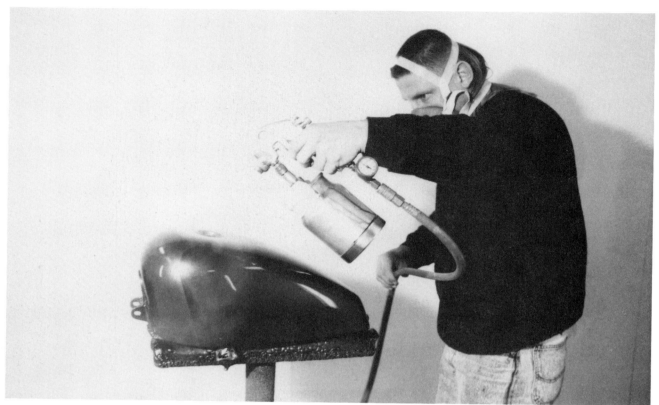

Mallard applies the topcoat in three medium wet coats. Second and third coats go on when the preceding coat is tack free. This is our candy coat, cobalt blue.

was pulled immediately after the application of the second coat. This way, the second base coat paint does not have enough time to bond to the tape and will not pull off with the tape.

PPG recommends that these base coat paints be topcoated between one and twenty-four hours after spraying. If the base coats are allowed to dry too long before topcoating, the topcoats do not adhere well enough. Again, the important point is to follow the manufacturer's recommendations for each product.

Three medium candy coats of Cobalt Blue resulted in the color we were looking for. These coats were sprayed fifteen minutes apart, when they were tack free. Because a candy coat shows the color underneath, modified by its own color, each candy coat changes the color and the look of the finished job. Spraying the recommended number of candy coats will give color like that on the color chart. You can always experiment with more or fewer coats (maybe on a spare fender?) for a more pleasing effect. In our case, three coats provided two deep blue tones and minimized the difference between the two base coats for a subtle two-tone effect.

Mallard applied one clear coat over the final candy coat with DAU 82 urethane clear twenty

minutes after spraying the last candy coat. After allowing this clear coat to dry overnight, we sanded it with 600-grit paper. Sanding the clear flattens out and eliminates any orange peel, eliminates dirt trapped at the surface, and leaves a scuffed surface for the pinstriping (the next step) to stick to. If we intended to follow this clear coat with more clear, then we would have used 800 or 1000 grit to flatten and smooth the surface. As a general rule with candy jobs and base coat/clear coat paint jobs, the sanding is always done on the clear coat, not on the base or candy coat.

The pinstriping of these parts is covered in Chapter 9. Following the pinstriping, Mallard applied three coats of the same urethane clear to protect the pinstripes and provide a great gloss to the tank and fenders.

If you are satisfied with the finish in the final clear coat, the job is finished. In our case, a few small imperfections showed up in the final clear coat. We sanded and polished them out of the paint job.

Polishing

It is sometimes hard to know whether or not to polish your new paint job. Mallard believes that there is no shine like the shine of new clear coat—

The almost-finished tank after the last coat of cobalt blue and one coat of clear. Different base colors can be seen through the candy coat. More coats of the candy would darken the color and minimize the difference between the two base coats.

without any polishing. For many of us, however, polishing is necessary as a means of eliminating a less than ideal finish or one that contains small particles of dust.

In the case of the Sportster, three little fish eyes appeared at the back of the tank. Because they went fairly deep, Mallard started with 1200-grit paper and a sponge. When most of the fish eyes were eliminated (without rubbing through to the paint underneath), he switched to 2000 grit (in most cases, you would start with the 2000-grit paper, not 1200).

After sanding the area with 2000 grit and eliminating the small impressions, Mallard started with a power buffer and some 3M polishing compound. The buffer pad was cotton and the speed was kept quite low. Satisfied that the sanding marks had been eliminated, it was time to switch to a special foam pad and liquid swirl remover. The special pad is designed to eliminate swirls and leave a perfectly polished surface.

After polishing the whole tank with the foam pad, we used a liquid wax, Liquid Lustre, and plenty of elbow grease as the final step. Most of these liquid wax products will help to eliminate

After all that work, we went and ruined the whole thing. Actually, we have to wet sand with 600 grit in order to create a surface the striping paint—our next step—will stick to. If we weren't striping, we could use 800 or 1000 grit to sand between clear coats.

The tank after sanding before it goes to the pinstriper. Sanding is always done on the clear coat and never on one of the color coats (see Chapter 9 for the pinstriping sequence).

After pinstriping, the tank was clear coated—and we found a few blemishes. The first step was to wet sand the imperfections with 1200-grit paper, because the imperfections were rather deep. This was followed by 2000-grit sandpaper. Next, a light polish from 3M was applied.

This is part of a system that typically starts with the 2000-grit wet sandpaper, progresses to the 3M polish used with a cotton cutting pad, and finishes with a 3M swirl remover on a separate finishing pad.

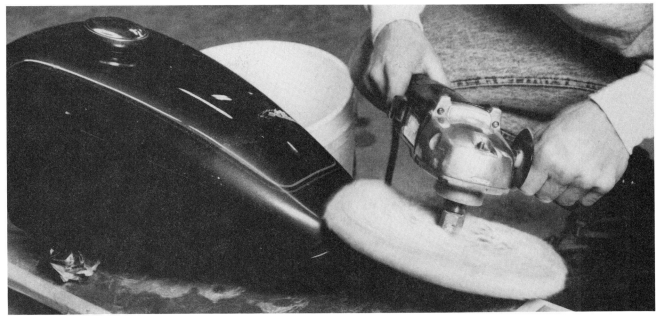

Mallard uses the polish with a cotton cutting pad, being careful to keep the speed low. If in doubt about using a *power buffer for the first time, don't. Work by hand instead.*

any lingering swirl marks and contain fillers for any tiny cracks or imperfections in the paint.

Just Do It

Although your own first paint job might be a little different than the one described here, the basic procedures are the same. The important thing is to convince yourself that you can do it—and then get out in that shop.

Mallard uses a liquid wax on a cotton towel as the final step. Most liquid waxes contain just a little cleaner that serves to further polish the surface. Always be careful to avoid rubbing through at an edge, even when working by hand with mild products.

The special final-polishing pad from 3M designed to eliminate any swirl marks and leave a perfect finish.

The finished product. Polishing leaves the clear coat with an incredible shine—though if the clear coat dries without any dust or imperfections, you could use the paint without the polishing step.

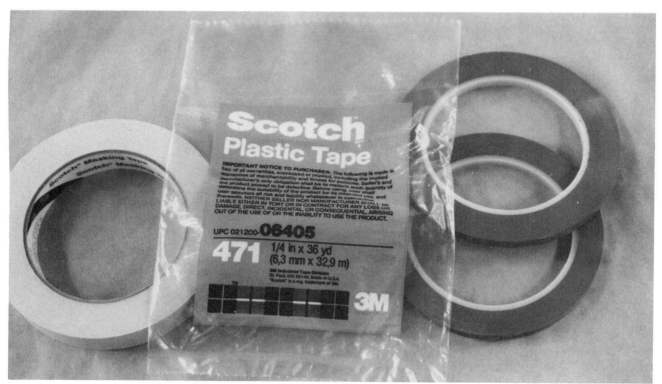

Plastic tape was used to tape out the design because it turns without tearing and does not wrinkle at the edge. A good quality 3/4in masking tape was used to provide a nice wide edge for the paper. Always buy good masking tape meant for automotive and motorcycle work—cheap tape might pull up the paint underneath.

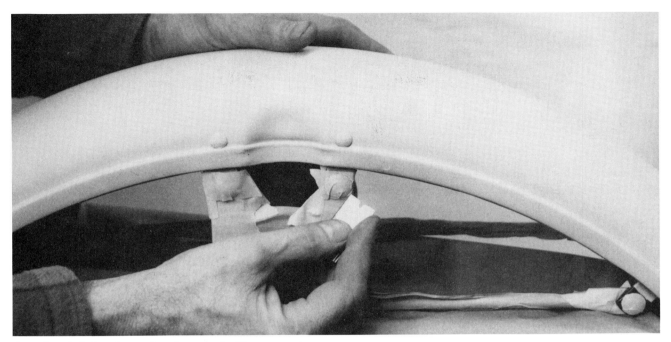

Stainless bolt heads are hard to mask. Here, we cover them with 3/4in tape then cut out the heads with a razor blade.

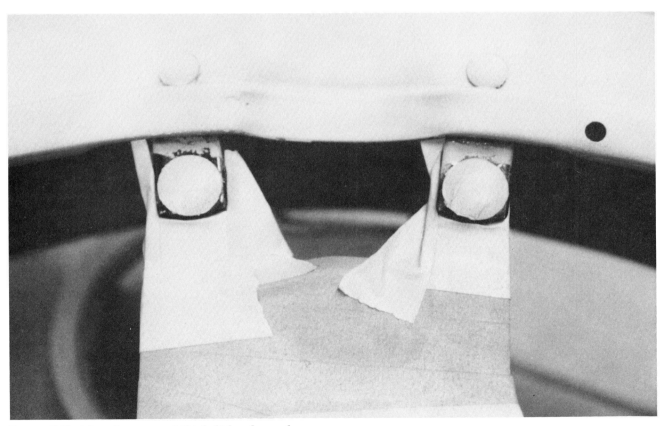

By carefully trimming around the bolt heads, we keep them shiny and unpainted.

Chapter 8

Two Custom Paint Jobs

From Start to Finish

Job Number 1:
The Master Does a Flame Job

The first project is a flame job done on a set of 3-1/2gal Fat Bob tanks and fenders. Flames always seem to be in style and no two flame jobs are the same. Flame jobs differ in the shape of the actual licks as well as the layout and materials used. You can create a traditional set of flames, with no overlap between each lick or you can design an elaborate set with overlapping licks. Colors can range from traditional white-yellow-red to blended candy or pearl base coat combinations, limited only by your imagination.

Design and Tape-out

The flame job seen here is the work of Jon Kosmoski. He makes it look easy—after all, he's

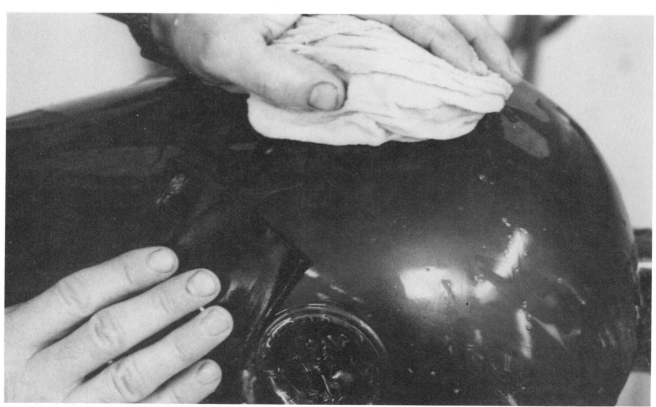

The start of the flame job by Jon Kosmoski. The tanks have been painted with Persimmon over an Orion Silver base, then covered with a clear coat. The clear coat is sanded with 500-grit sandpaper before the tape-out be- *gins. Jon recommends using high-quality sandpaper as the size of the grains is more consistent than with brand-X papers.*

Jon Kosmoski does all his designing on the tank, determining the layout as he goes. The tape is 1/8in masking tape. Slight differences from one side to the other are not noticeable, except on top of the tanks where you can see both at once. Anytime Jon does not like the way a flame is going, he just pulls the tape up and starts over.

been doing this for thirty-seven years. The tanks were first painted with Orion Silver base, then topcoated with a mixture of candy tangerine and candy apple red (to produce a color Jon calls persimmon). Two coats of clear (a bond coat and one heavier coat) have been sprayed on top of the persimmon candy paint. The first step is a good wet sanding the next day with 500-grit paper. The sanding is done on the clear coat to give the flame paint a good surface to stick to.

After scuffing the surface with the sandpaper, Jon starts the tape-out. He does not use any kind of grease pencil and designs right on the metal. He suggests that if you design on paper, start out with pictures of the tanks. "You can always take pictures of the tanks," he said, "blow up the pictures on the copy machine, and try different flame designs until you find something you like. People can even draw the flames out full size and trace that design onto the tank."

Jon uses conventional masking tape from a roll only 1/8in thick. He reports that his Shimrin base coats have almost no tendency to migrate under the edge of the tape. Using the nonplastic tape with another company's base coats might not work so well. His design for this Harley calls for long flowing flames, a design that he says, "will make the bike look longer—this thing will look like it's moving when it's standing still."

Jon starts at one end of one tank and designs as he goes. If he does not like the shape of a partic-

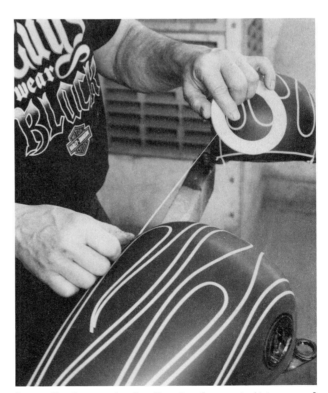

Jon pulls the tape in the direction he wants it to go and guides it with his thumb. If the tape breaks, he splices in a new piece (never splice-in a curve, however). Jon makes sure his hands are clean before he starts and touches the tanks as little as possible during the tape-out.

After the 1/8in tape is in place, Jon fills the area outside the flame with 3/4in tape. Like the sandpaper, the tape should be a brand name item meant for automotive and motorcycle work.

ular flame, he pulls the tape up and starts over. If the tape breaks (which it sometimes does), he splices in new tape, cautioning first-time painters to never splice the tape in a curve because it will show there.

When Jon is satisfied with the flame layout on one tank, he starts on the other side. Tracing paper and a pounce wheel (a special marking device available at art stores) could be used to transfer the shape exactly, though most artists use their eye—with help from a small tape measure—to duplicate the design from one tank to the other. Jon pointed out the importance of getting the tops of the two tanks the same, as you can see both at the same time when seated on the bike.

When Jon starts on the fenders, he marks the center with a thin strip of tape. This makes it much easier to keep the two sides balanced. The tape-out on the fenders, especially the front fenders (this customer sent two front fenders for one bike) was designed to mirror the shape of the flames on the tanks, and features long flowing flame licks.

On the rear fender, Jon demonstrated a neat trick: He taped a template to the fender to show the location of the taillight; two strips of tape show the position of the fender struts. This makes it

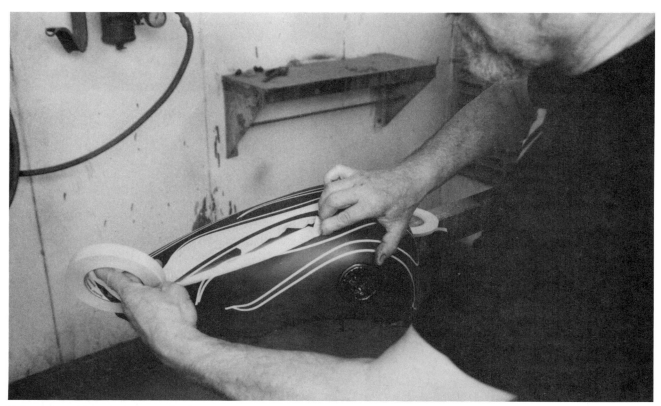

Using the wider tape is much the same as using the 1/8in tape—pull it the way you want it to go and guide it with your thumb. Jon warns against asking one piece of tape to change direction too many times because too many wrinkles are created.

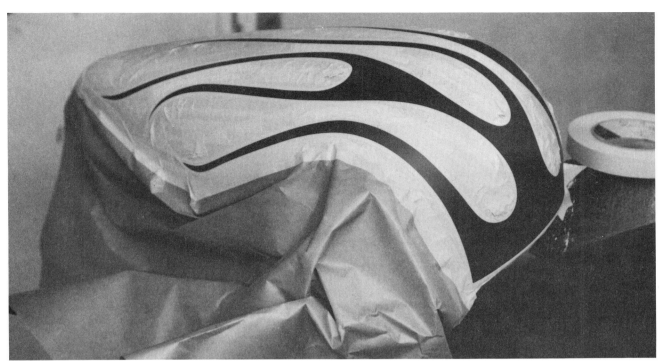

When the flames are completely taped out, you can really see the shape of the design. Don't hesitate to pull the tape and change a design or a flame lick that does not seem right.

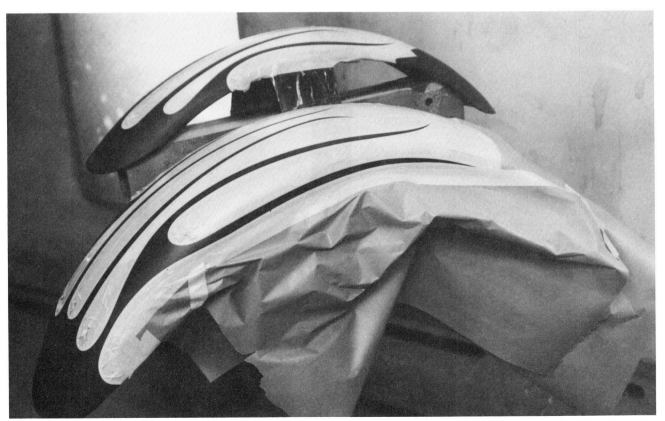

The two front fenders after all the taping is finished. Note the long flowing flame licks. A flame or scallop design needs to be consistent from one part of the bike to the next.

much easier to design and lay out a flame design that will look good on the assembled fender.

After all the parts were taped-out with the 1/8in tape, Jon and Denny Christenson filled in the open areas with 3/4in tape. Masking paper was used to fill the larger areas. The 3/4in tape is laid on to cover half the thin tape and is applied starting at the front of each area that must be masked. By carefully applying the tape from front to rear, and overlapping the edges, the masking tape can be applied so it all comes off with one pull from the front when the job is done. Pulling it all off at once is much easier than picking off each individual piece of tape.

Once the parts are completely taped off, you can see the shape of the flames. This is another good opportunity to critique the job—it is easier to change it now than after the parts are painted (though Jon's Shimrin base coats can be wiped off with solvent up to one hour after application if they have been sprayed over a urethane).

Time for Paint—Finally

Although the preparation always seems to take too long, after all the taping we are ready for paint. Jon decided to create the flames in multi-colored pearls, so the first step is a good base color. After wiping down the area to be painted with a tack rag, Jon sprayed two medium coats of white base coat, BC-26. These paints dry quickly, and after less than ten minutes we are ready to start with the multi-colored flames.

Jon painted the beginning of the flames with Sunrise Pearl—a warm yellow pearl color sprayed on the front of the tanks and the first part of each flame lick. After three medium coats of yellow, he used an orange pearl color, called Tangelo, for the next stage in these multi-colored flames. This orange color was sprayed farther back on each flame lick and used to darken parts of the yellow on the front of the tanks. At this point, it becomes convenient to keep a touch-up paint gun handy; that gun will put a narrow fan of yellow or orange right where you want it.

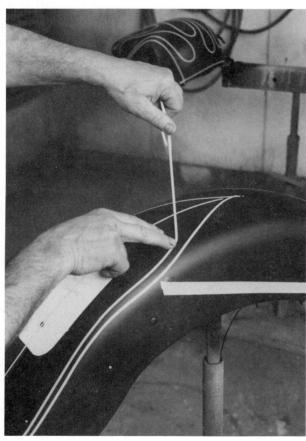

Jon tapes off the rear fender. It is hard to duplicate the look of the other parts as so little of the fender is actually available for flaming. Again, the tape is pulled with one hand and guided with the other. Note that the fender's exact center has been marked with another piece of tape that will be removed later.

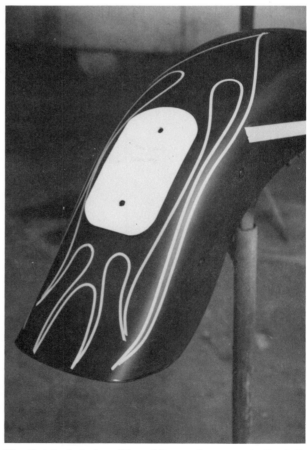

The finished design. The white card represents the taillight while the horizontal strip of tape represents the fender strut—it is much easier to design the flames when you know where these parts are.

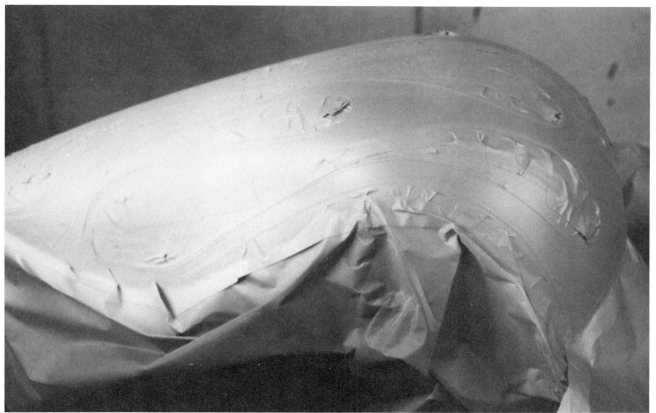

The flames will be done in pearls, so the first step was two coats of BC 26 base coat, a white that gives the pearls a nice glow. Next comes two coats of Sunrise Pearl (a warm yellow color) sprayed over the white base at the front of the tanks. The finished flames will be four colors, fading from yellow to orange, to pink and then blue at the tips.

The next color is Hot Pink Pearl, added near the end of each flame lick. Again, three medium coats were applied. Of note, neither these paints nor the white base coats contain any isocyanates so we were able to spray wearing only a charcoal-type of respirator.

The final color is a lavender used at the flame tips. It is sprayed in three medium coats and blended with the pink that went on farther up the tank.

The tape can be pulled right away to avoid picking up any paint with the tape or leaving a tape mark where the tape was laid down. "This is where the careful taping pays off," Jon explained, "because each area can be pulled clean in one fell swoop." Following the removal of the masking paper and 3/4in tape, the 1/8in tape was pulled, being careful to avoid picking up any fresh paint along with the tape.

The almost-final steps are the three clear coats sprayed on all the parts. The clear was done in three coats, with one light "tack" coat followed by two medium coats. After drying, the clear coats were sanded with 500-grit paper. Pinstriping will

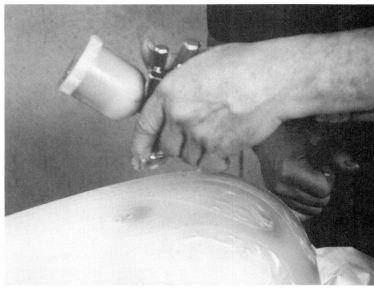

Jon uses a Binks HVLP touch-up gun to darken the edges of the Sunrise Yellow with Tangelo Pearl (an orange color). The gun is cleaned and flushed thoroughly between color changes.

Interview:
Jon Kosmoski of House of Kolor

Jon Kosmoski is a legend in the paint business. What's especially great about Jon is the fact that he is not sitting behind a desk directing a bunch of underlings to do this or that; he is still working in the paint booth, trying new materials, colors, and techniques. Dressed in his trademark black T-shirt, jeans, and cowboy boots, Jon always finds time to answer questions or help customers and paint suppliers with questions.

Jon got his start working as a mechanic after high school. He often found himself painting cars and motorcycles after punching out at his day job, however. John opened his first shop in the early 1960s. He remembers that it had six work stalls and no bathroom. "We had to use the bathroom at the bar up the alley." Family responsibilities meant that Jon had to keep the full time mechanic's job for a while and work in his own shop at night. By the late 1960s, the body and paint shop had enough business that Jon was able to quit his day job and concentrate full time on painting and body work.

It was the paint industry's change over to acrylic lacquer in the late 1950s that lead Jon to his current status as a paint manufacturer. The new materials were much better technically, but did not have any of the wonderful colors that Jon and other custom painter's had created with the older nitrocellulose lacquers. Jon figured there had to be a better way (or at least a better color). Soon, he was working with a chemist and reading chemistry books at night, trying to create acrylic lacquers with the bright colors of the older nitro-based materials.

Today, Jon is still looking for that illusive better color. As the industry moves toward reduced VOCs and nonlead based pigments, constant changes and challenges confront a quality paint manufacturer like Jon Kosmoski. I once said that if everyone had as much enthusiasm for what they do as Jon Kosmoski, the world would be a better place. After interviewing him, that statement still rings true. Jon is truly a man doing his best and loving every minute of it.

My interview with Jon ran a little long, but then Jon has much to say. What follows is an hour spent with Jon Kosmoski, talking about his favorite subject—paint and custom painting.

Tell us about some of your first bikes and the early custom paint jobs you did.

When I started riding in 1955, it was on Limey bikes. My first bike was a BSA Golden Flash, it had the chrome tank sides so I didn't do much to that. Next, I had an Aerial Square Four. It was when I bought my Matchless Typhoon that I started getting into painting bikes. I did a flame job on that bike. That was a great bike, I wish I still had it.

So, I mean my whole painting career started by painting motorcycle tanks and helmets for friends. The paint was all nitrocellulose lacquer in those days so the gas would mess with it, but it was all we had. We didn't have two-part primers, so there were some problems. Then we started using pearls and candies.

People act like a tri-coat system [base coat, candy or pearl coat, and then clear coat] is a new deal; we were doing that a long time ago. Candies and pearls are both tri-coat systems. There weren't that many Harleys around back then. I didn't get into painting the whole motorcycle until later, when the chopper thing happened.

By the late 1960s, we had grown to the point where we did 500 sets of motorcycle parts from November to April. We had a real production system set up so we could get all the work done and keep track of everybody's parts. We had one or two guys who did nothing but molding—it was quite a system we had set up.

You always emphasize preparing the parts. What should be done? Where do people make mistakes in their prep work?

I have this saying, "If you paint over another paint job—other than a factory job—your reputation depends on that other person's paint job." So if you don't have knowledge of that paint job you are painting over, strip it off. It's so simple to get out a can of stripper and get off the old paint and put on a good two-part epoxy primer that's going to be an excellent bond to the metal. Something that will give you some longevity. One of the reasons Von Dutch got out of paint jobs was he didn't like the way they didn't last. He wanted more permanent paint jobs. And it was impossible back in those nitrocellulose days. I mean, if gasoline would wash the paint off, and it would, how good was that paint? A guy's bike would tip over and you could see where the gas had run down the tank and taken off the paint or at least stained it. Not with the new coating systems. The stuff is impervious to fuel, even nitromethane fuel. All Nitro does to our UC 1 clear is dull the finish, a buffer brings the shine right back.

Today, if you are spraying over a factory finish, I see nothing wrong with cleaning the surface and sanding it down good and simply sealing it. Use spot putty (preferably the two-part putties) if you have chips that go down to the metal and use lacquer primer in those areas where it went down to metal. But use a good sealer and then paint. You've got to use a good sealer and you've got to read the label. Painters don't want to read those labels. There's a window; you have to wait so long after spraying the sealer, but if you wait too long then you have to sand it and apply another coat of sealer. The paint will only bond to the sealer during a certain period of time.

How important is shop temperature?

Well, when I say wait so long to apply the next coat, I'm assuming the shop is at least 70 degrees. People call me and say they sprayed the paint and put on the clear the next day and the clear lifted. Then I say, how hot was the shop? They say it was seventy. I say, did you leave the heat on overnight? And they say no, the heat was turned off and the shop went down to 40 degrees. So the cool temperature acted like a retarder and nothing cured properly.

One of the biggest problems we have is people painting in shops where it's only 60 degrees. If you are a painter and you pay attention to solvent release from the paint film, 2 degrees makes a major difference in the way the solvents evaporate from the film. If I'm in a shop that's 72 degrees, that's a good environment—assuming all the reducers are correct for that temperature.

The other problem that these guys at home have is the air movement in their little shop. Most motorcycle parts are painted in open rooms. Even if you are at 85 degrees, you aren't moving any air past that part. Air movement is what pulls the solvents out of the paint. I tell people, if they're in an open room, go to the next fastest reducer or thinner. A booth will move fifty to one-hundred lineal feet of air per minute. Think about how much air is moving past that object. People don't realize this. It was about ten years before I realized this. I'd go into the store and get the high-gloss thinner and I was working in a 65-degree shop—I wanted high gloss but I never read the label and didn't know the thinner was designed to be used at 85 degrees. In effect, I was putting paint remover on the parts and I'd spray and spray and I'd wonder why the candies were soaking down into the base. In those lacquer jobs, I was sliding the whole thing off the side of the tank or fenders.

The other factor that comes in is humidity. If it's a humid day, you are not going to get the evaporation that you would on a drier day, so you've got to take that into account. Lacquers will blush on a day with high humidity.

The other problem that people have is trapping solvents between coats. You go into a shop and some guy is spraying lacquer primer and then blowing air over it to speed up the drying. He sees the surface finish change and thinks that the paint is dry, but it isn't. What he's actually doing is skinning the surface and trapping solvents in the paint below that skin.

If the paint can says acrylic, think of it as a sheet of plastic wrap. Painters put one coat on top of another without allowing it to dry sufficiently. And then when the vehicle is parked in the sun the job turns to mush—solvents trapped under the top coat eventually work their way to the top and cause a problem, blush, or de-lamination.

Tell us about properly applying primer.

I think a lot of painters screw up on the paint bench. Number one, they don't stir the individual components and they don't measure, they rely on their eyeball. They don't treat the primer with respect. They say that they'll just sand it down and everything will come out OK, but they're making more work for themselves.

They don't strain the primer. If there's an incubation time, they must follow that activation time. Painters should read the labels before they start so they really understand the products.

How do you get the primer flat so the final paint job looks good and has a good shine?

It's hard to block sand bikes because the parts are so curvey. A flexible pad is a good idea. A guide coat is a real good idea. A guide coat is one of the few times I use lacquer primer. After spraying on the two-part primer, I put on a light coat of contrasting lacquer primer and then start the sanding. Any low spots or pits show up right away as dark spots that weren't sanded off. This is a good way to check yourself as you go along.

People must read directions. On metal etch, a lot of people use it straight when it should be diluted. And they don't clean the metal afterwards and so leave a residue behind [a few products are meant to be left on] that causes problems later.

Can your two-part primers be used on bare steel without using a metal etch first?

Yes, but the metal must be clean and dry. I hate to see guys holding the tank with one hand and sanding with the other. The hand holding the tank will leave oils behind and those oils won't do anything to aid the adhesion of the paint—no matter whose paint it is. Preparation is the key to longevity.

What do people do wrong when it comes to body work?

One of the big problems is plastic filler that isn't curing correctly. They don't knead the hardener before they mix it with the filler. That hardener is benzoil peroxide. Sometimes you open the tube and get pure water-like liquid coming out—that's pure benzoil peroxide—that's what causes bleeding through in the paint job. I put mine in the refrigerator so the materials in the tube don't separate. If I can feel the little seeds in the tube of hardener, I throw it out and get another tube.

I mix the filler well, but try not to whip it so as to get air bubbles. I apply it as close to the final shape as I can—why make more work for yourself? Why put on a lot of material you know you are going to have to sand off?

Should people use no-stain bondo when the paint is a light color?

Yes, the stuff definitely works. The hardener in the no-stain is a ketone instead of benzoil peroxide. They've got stain-free spot putties now, too—two-part putties that are much better than the old lacquer-based putties. Bondo underneath three coats of our epoxy primer won't bleed through. But what if you block sand the primer and you find a low spot? Well, you should use a no-stain putty or filler on that low spot and cover the area with lacquer primer—then you can finish the job that day.

What grit of sandpaper do I need to use before applying final paint?

I think you need to sand the two-part primer with 400-grit wet, or 240 if you use a double-action sander. Topcoats adhere through a combination of chemical and mechanical bonding. I recommend that people sand well for a good mechanical bond.

Do people need to use a sealer?

A sealer improves the adhesion between the topcoat and primer if the label is followed. A sealer makes the primer closer to the color you are applying. It's available in different colors; you need to use the one that's close to your final color. It also contains a compound called berrides, which prevents solvent movement so you do not move solvents from the topcoat to the primer layers [if you use two-part primer, you probably don't need this chemical resistance to solvent movement because most two-part primers are solvent resistant].

People in the industry talk about color hold-out. How does sealer improve hold-out?

The sealer prevents the final color from soaking down into the primer, so the color that you see in the finish coat is the same color as the one on the paint card. If part of the paint soaks into the primer, shrinkage and loss of gloss can occur sometimes months after the job is finished.

What are some other do's and don'ts?

Use a timer. I use a sixty minute timer to measure dry times between coats and incubation times. I never guess at any of that.

You can't cross-mix components between one company and another. You can't use one company's hardener with another's paint, or use one firm's clear over another's urethane or lacquer.

There's much talk about urethanes being the paints of the future, but they're toxic. Can painters use urethanes in a home shop? How careful do people have to be with these products?

Unless these people have set up their shops with correct ventilation and use an air supply respirator with an oil-less compressor supplying fresh air to the hood, they should stay away from these products. They also need to wear gloves and a complete painter's suit.

Jon Kosmoski during a break in the paint booth.

These materials are toxic and must be handled with care. I do know guys who buy sheets of poly, drape it, and create a small booth in the garage. They have squirrel-cage blowers to provide some ventilation and then rent or buy a fresh-air hood and compressor. The compressor for the fresh-air hood must be set outside the booth where it can draw fresh air. I like to get it up off the floor, because paint vapors tend to be heavy and stay near the floor. Painters must remember that if the fresh-air compressor is picking up fumes and recycling them, they've defeated the whole purpose of the mask and compressor.

Are lacquers durable? When will they be phased out due to concerns about VOCs?

I think we'll have lacquer for at least ten years, except for certain areas like California. In terms of the reputation lacquer has for cracking, most cracks are due to poor preparation or the use of a cheap primer. Lacquer primers are brittle and some of the cracking in lacquer is due to the primer. I painted a Corvette fifteen years ago with acrylic lacquer and the paint job looks like it's no more than one year old, there isn't one crack. So the new acrylic lacquers—at least our own—are flexible, but you've got to use a real quality two-part primer underneath the lacquer.

Lacquer—again, I can only speak for our own product—will be softened by gasoline spills. When you remove the gas, the paint recovers. So a little spill at the gas station won't hurt our lacquer at all. Even in a situation where the bike falls over, the gas won't wash off the paint unless the bike stays there for a long time with gas running over the paint.

Can people who work at home and who don't want to mess with urethanes because of the isocyanates use lacquer?

Yes, they can use our base coats, they contain no isocyanates. Then they can topcoat them with lacquer candies and lacquer clear coats.

Where do people get in trouble with topcoats and finish coats?

Especially with lacquer, once you start a job, it's essential that you finish it within forty-eight hours—that's from the first topcoat or candy coat to the last coat. In cases where the job calls for multiple tape-outs and you want to work from weekend to weekend—well, you just can't. What you have to do is put a coat of clear on to "keep the job open" for another forty-eight hours. Acrylic lacquer, when it dries, is like a sheet of plastic that's been shrunk to the object. When it's dry like that and then you spray on fresh paint with fresh solvents, the solvents attack that sheet of plastic. There's a release of that tension and you can get crow's-feet cracks.

People need to understand what a bond coat is. It means a light, wet coat with a restricted trigger pull, that you let sit for five minutes. That light film of paint will stick to the paint underneath and make a good surface for the next coat of paint to stick to. This reduces runs and fish eyes.

With enamels, you always need a bond coat [urethanes are considered an enamel], lacquers aren't as critical. I tell people to use a touch test. If the paint strings when you pull your finger off, then the paint is still flowing and you can't paint on top of something that's flowing.

Guys should always use a test panel, so the gun is correctly adjusted when they start on the motorcycle or car. And they've got to keep the guns clean. If the pattern doesn't look quite right, clean that air cap and fluid tip with a little brush and try again.

Gun adjustment is real important. I never narrow the pattern. I start with the material knob turned in to close and opened up about two turns, and then I check the pattern. I leave the upper knob wide open. I only turn down the upper knob [air to the horns] when I over-reduce the material to get back to an even oval or when I'm trying to spray in restricted areas.

Is there anything else painters should be aware of?

Yes, painters have to draw imaginary straight lines or a grid over the object and follow those with the gun. You can't let each pass across the tank turn down at the end and converge at the back of the tank. You have to imagine those straight lines. At the ends or corners, you use a banding pass to fill those areas because, of course, the paint won't turn corners.

People should tape off the filler area; the gasket from the gas cap should sit on bare metal. If you've got paint on the area where the cap seals, use a razor blade or wire brush to clean that area. Some of the new Harleys have that area painted, but they're using some new, powder-clear, a super-paint that resists gas. With most other paints, you want that area clean so the fumes can't work up from the tank and under the paint film to cause a blister near the fill area.

be done on this clear coat and then more clear will be added to protect the pinstripes.

Jon chose to do his own pinstriping, using a Mack 00 brush and light blue urethane pinstriping paint (from House of Kolor, of course). A better look at the pinstriping is included in Chapter 9. After the urethane pinstriping paint had dried, Jon applied two coats of clear. After those clear coats had dried overnight, he sanded with 500 grit, and sprayed on two additional coats of clear. These

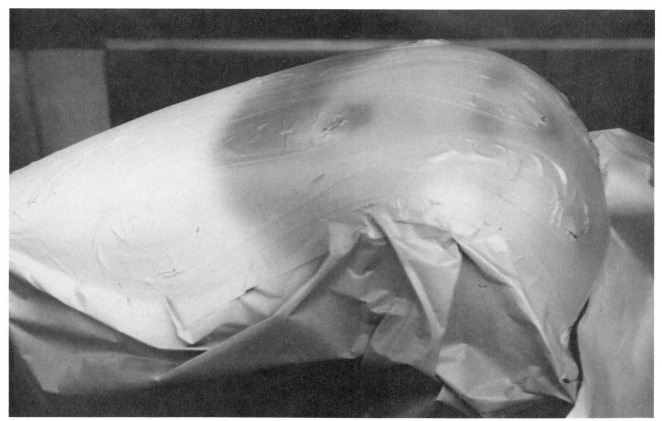

More of the Tangelo—the second color in the four-color flame job—has been sprayed on the tank. It is important to apply the paint evenly and from more than one angle because of the small ridges created by the masking tape.

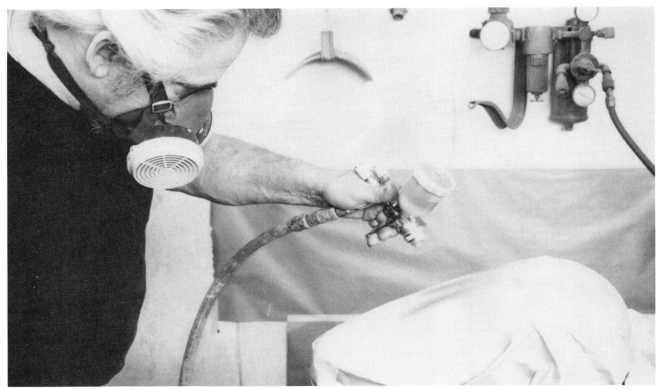

Jon applies the Hot Pink Pearl, the third color. Blending the colors smoothly so they flow, from yellow through orange and pink to the lavender tips, is an art that requires practice.

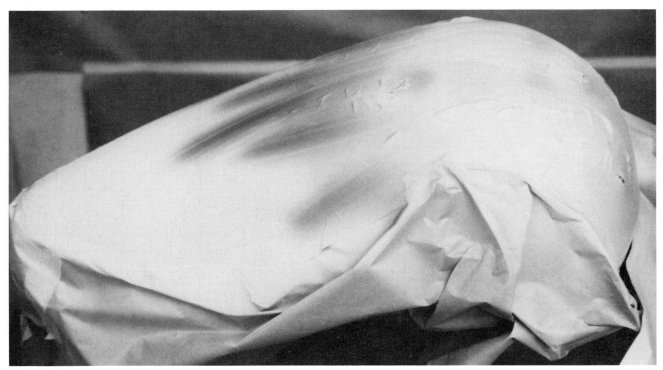

A better look at the blend from yellow to orange to Hot Pink (yes, it would be nice to do all this in color, but then you might have to pay twice as much for the book).

last two (extra) coats of clear were over-reduced per the instructions on the cans. The extra coats of clear were added to give the parts a superior shine. As the last step, Jon went through a polishing sequence, starting with 2000-grit paper, progressing through a liquid polish, and finishing with a swirl remover.

Job Number 2:
A Painter Paints His Own Bike

Mallard Teal paints many motorcycles. When it came time to paint his own bike, it seemed natural that he would want something special—a paint job even more colorful than the great jobs he does for his customers.

The first step was the removal of all the old paint. Next, Mallard painted everything with DP 50 from PPG, a good catalyzed primer. Because the sheet metal was in good condition, Mallard did not do any filling and went from the primer right to the base coats.

Mallard decided to do a scallop job, with aqua scallops on a purple base. Using the side covers as his test panels, he started with Purple Velvet (all the materials are from the PPG line) and Light

Aqua scallops. That combination didn't seem quite right, so he added black shadows to the scallops. Mallard liked the shadows but the purple didn't seem like the right shade and the aqua looked too green.

To give the purple a richer look, Mallard created a tinted clear (you could call this a light candy coat) made up of Candy Romanesque Crimson diluted with clear. Three light coats of this on top of the purple created a reddish tint and made the purple look much richer. The Light Aqua was tinted in the same way, but with Candy Grandeur Blue mixed with clear and sprayed over the aqua.

Creating tinted clears might be more work than most amateur painters want to do, but it illustrates the idea that you do not have to use the paints as they come from the can. Experiment a little, create your own candy coat; try a new combination of base color and candy that is not on the paint card.

The actual paint job started by painting all the parts in the Purple Velvet, first a light coat for good adhesion and then a heavier coat. After the second coat was tack free, Mallard applied light mist coats of the tinted clear. The tinted clear was

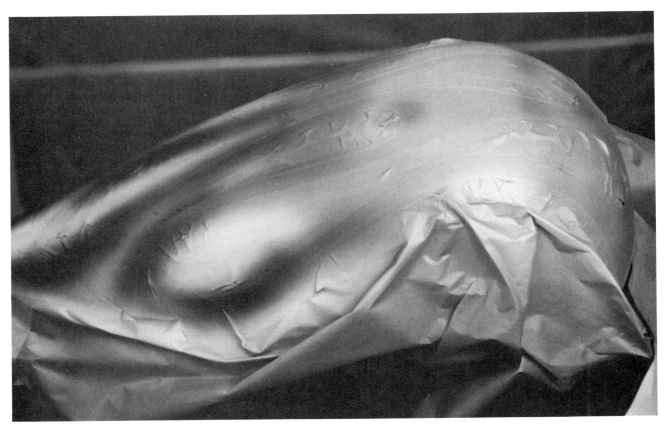

Almost finished. Here the tank has been sprayed with all four colors, including the lavender tips. The clear coats, pinstriping, and more clear coats are yet to be completed.

Jon applied the 3/4in tape in such a fashion that the whole piece could be pulled at once—making the job of tape removal easy and fast.

applied in light coats in order to ensure that the coverage was even. "It is easy to get a blotchy effect when using a tinted clear coat," Mallard warned. "You've got to be sure that the coverage is even."

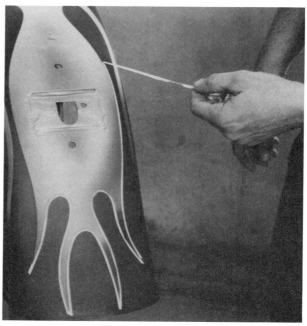

The finished rear fender. Note that the tape is pulled away from the paint at an angle to the side—the idea is to get the tape to pull away clean and minimize any tendency to lift the fresh paint.

The tank after the tape has been removed. Pinstripes will cover up small imperfections at the edge.

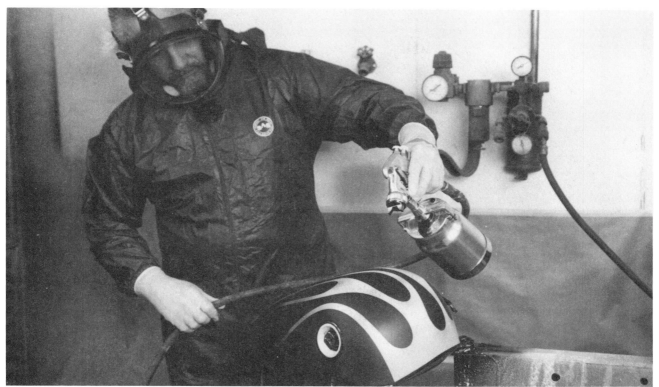

Pinstripes are done on the clear coat. Jon applies a catalyzed clear urethane; note the full mask with fresh air supply and the painter's coveralls. Jon's base coats, however, contain no isocyanates and do not require a fresh-air hood.

Jon puts on clear in three coats—first a light bond coat, then two heavier coats. Remember that some of the clear will be sanded off, limiting the total film thickness.

True custom painting like this requires painters to use their eye to judge what is right. Mallard judged the color to be right after putting four coats of tinted clear over the Purple Velvet.

After the tinted clear coats had dried twenty-four hours, it was time to start the tape-outs. In his typical fashion, Mallard designed the scallops on the tank, using plastic tape from 3M. He marked the center of the tank with a small strip of tape at the top and started the tape-out, working from the center out toward the edge. When all the scallops were laid out, the spacing did not seem right so Mallard pulled the tape and changed the spacing on the side of the tank. If doing this all by eye seems rather intimidating, use a small tape measure to double check dimensions. When the scallops were arranged to his satisfaction, Mallard taped off the rest of the tank with 3/4in masking tape and masking paper.

Normally, a piece like the tank would be wiped down with a cleaner before applying another color or a clear coat. Because of the tape and the fact that the tape would hold any solvents used in cleaning, Mallard ran a tack rag over the surface before beginning to spray the Light Aqua.

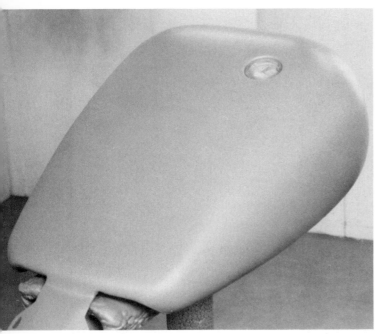

Mallard's tank in primer—clean and smooth and ready for the Purple Velvet base coat.

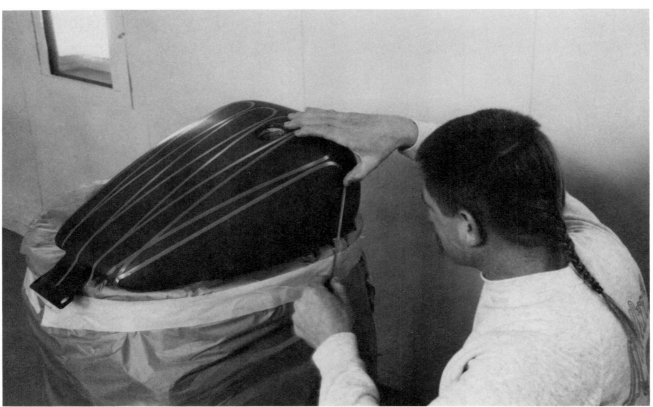

After the base coats and tinted clear coats, Mallard Teal designs the layout directly on the metal, working with neither a sketch nor drawing. 3M plastic tape was used to shape these scallops. Creating a smooth curve takes *practice. Mallard uses his thumb in combination with his other hand to create the right shape. He makes sure his hands are clean and that he minimizes contact between his hands and the tank so no oils are transferred.*

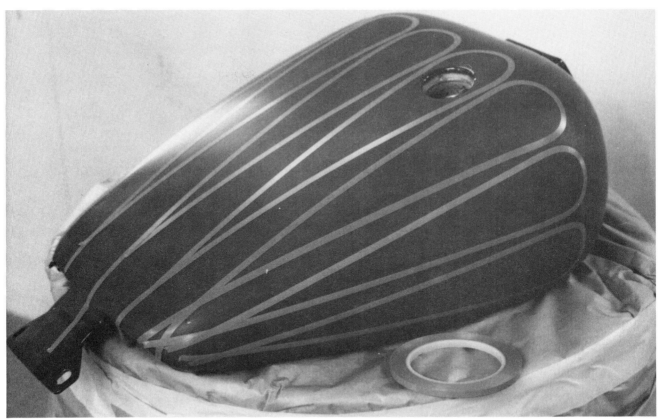

Spacing of the scallops took three tries before it was right. A small tape measure can be used, along with a keen eye, to make sure spacing is even and equal from side to side.

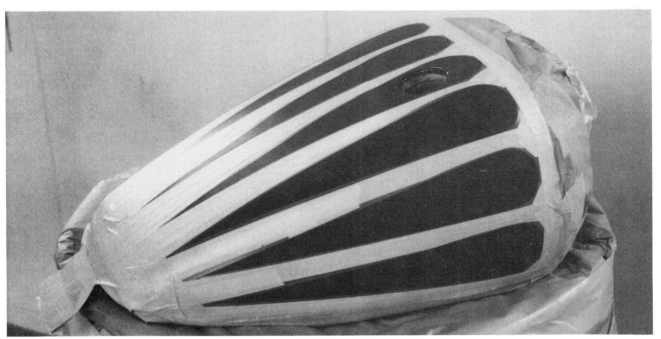

Three-quarter inch masking tape is used to fill the spaces between the plastic tape. Make sure that the tape over-laps and that it is stuck tightly to the tank. Ready for the Light Aqua, this tank will be cleaned with a tack rag before the spraying starts. Because of the tape, solvents or lacquer thinner cannot be used for cleaning.

Mallard applied three coats of Light Aqua, a light tack coat, and two medium coats. Next, he re-taped the scallop area, leaving only the shadow exposed. Then it was time to apply two coats of black (the lavender, aqua, and black are all DBU base coat colors).

With only the scallop (both the aqua and the black) untaped, Mallard started the tinting process. As stated, the tint used was Candy Grandeur Blue diluted with clear, sprayed in light coats over the Light Aqua scallops. Three coats of the tinted clear gave a blue tint to the aqua, exactly the effect Mallard wanted. Because the tint was so light, there was no noticeable effect on the black part of the scallop.

Mallard immediately untaped the parts and, after waiting until the last tint coat was tack free, he sprayed two coats of clear (DBU 88) over all the parts. He sanded this coat, striped it (see Chapter 9), then cleared again.

Have Spray Gun, Will Travel

Two different paint jobs were described here. Each painter used different materials and meth-

Mallard puts on the first coat of Light Aqua that will form the scallops. This is a DBU base coat without any isocyanates.

Three coats of the Light Aqua (one bond coat and two medium coats) give good coverage of the scallops.

108

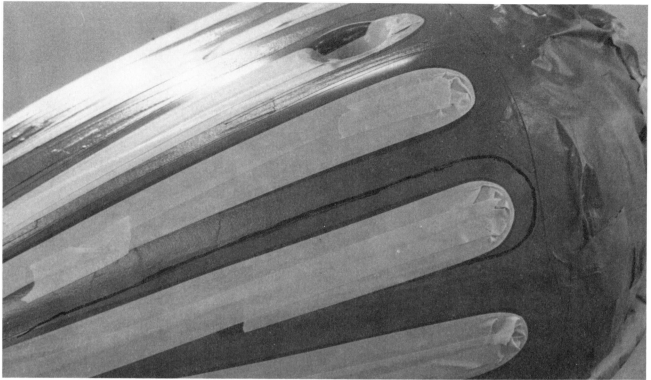

Now the job gets confusing. After the Light Aqua dries, it is taped over, leaving just the shadow that will be painted in black. One of these areas has been outlined to make it easier to see.

After two coats of black, Mallard has good coverage. At this point it looks like a mess—but it will all make sense when the tape comes off.

ods; each achieved different effects. The two jobs illustrate the fact that you can paint almost anything you can imagine on a motorcycle.

Custom painting is just that—custom. No two paint jobs are quite the same because no two painters are the same. The only thing custom painters have in common is a thorough understanding of the materials and a willingness to try something new.

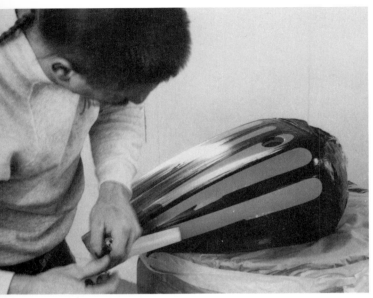

After the scallops are untaped—both the Light Aqua and the black shadow—they will be sprayed with clear tinted with Grandeur Blue to give the aqua a deeper hue. The tinted clear will not affect the color of the black.

The finished tank with the scallops and carefully laid out shadows, all covered in clear. The only thing left is to scuff the tank, pinstripe the scallops, and apply clear coat again.

Chapter 9

Pinstripes and Special Effects

Maximum Impact From Minimal Paint

Pinstriping is a small, though necessary, part of any custom paint job. Though we tend to think of pinstripes as accents to a complete paint job or the outlines of a fancy flame job, pinstripes can *become* the paint job (check the paint Lenny Schwartz put on the Sportster tank to fully understand what can be done with pinstripes).

If you are going to let the professional pinstriper do the work, rely on him or her for help with the design. If you are going to do the pinstriping yourself, plan out a good design before you start in with the paint.

Designing Your Pinstripes

When considering the stripes that best fit your bike, remember that in most cases pinstripes are used as accents. This is a case where less is usually more. It is easy to brush on more and more

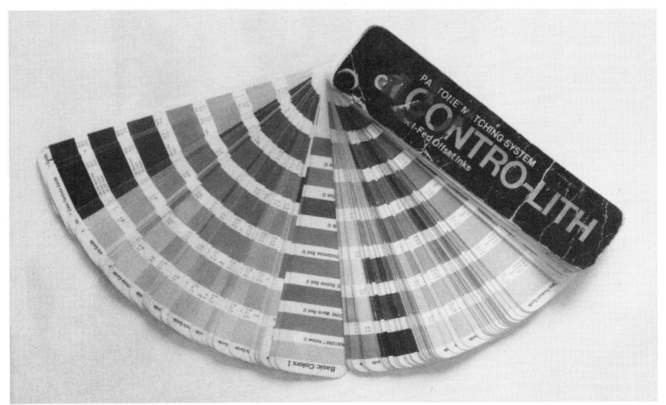

The Pantone Matching System (PMS) is a book used by commercial printers to select colors. The book can be found at most art supply houses, and it's a great way to compare two or three colors to see how they match. You can also hold one color up against the color on your tank to judge the effect.

paint, but not so easy to neatly brush on a tasteful design.

Designing your stripes means picking both a design and the colors for the stripes themselves. In general, you need contrast between the pinstripes and the colors they go over or outline. If it is a traditional set of flames you are striping, you might want to use a traditional cobalt blue. The subtle two-tone blue paint on the Sportster seen in this book was striped in two shades of violet. Unless you have an eye for color, choosing an appropriate color can be the toughest part of the job.

Help is available in the form of a paint card. Try holding the chips up against the paint on your bike or two chips next to each other to see how they work together. Some painters use a Pantone Matching System (PMS) booklet filled with colors intended for a commercial printer. These little booklets of color are available from graphic arts supply houses and will help you choose one or two colors that will have just the right punch when applied over your new paint job.

The visual impact of the stripes is increased dramatically if you use two colors. These colors are often related, though the actual choice is up to you. Two colors usually provide about four times the impact.

Materials

Sometimes, the only way to find the right color combination is to try a certain color on the bike. This is easy to do as most striping paints can be wiped off with a dry rag or one dipped in thinner, up to an hour or more after application.

The paints used for striping fall into two categories, striping enamel or striping urethane. All of these paints are designed to be inert, meaning they are meant to go on over other paints without any reaction between the two paints. The two enamels most commonly used are One Shot sign-painting enamel and Chromatic lettering enamel. Though the One Shot seems to be the most common, the Chromatic offers a wider range of colors. Both are enamels and both can be easily wiped off if you make a mistake.

Brian Truesdell of St. Paul, Minnesota, uses either One Shot or Chromatic striping paint. Both are inert enamels, designed to be painted onto other paints without creating any reaction between the two. His brushes come from Mack and are made from squirrel or camel hair.

If you cannot find the color you want, mix two colors to get the right one. Brian uses small Dixie cups for mixing because they do not have any wax coating.

Jon Kosmoski's House of Kolor offers the only true urethane striping paint, available in his usual wide array of super-bright colors. It can be applied as a topcoat with catalyst or used without a catalyst if you intend to clear coat the stripes.

Pinstripes are usually applied with those funny looking brushes that have the short handles and the long, long bristles. Good ones are made of camel or squirrel hair, though synthetics are slowly replacing the natural fibers. Striping brushes are rated by size, starting at five for a large brush and going to zero or double-zero for very fine work. Some stripers cut half the bristles out of a double-zero to get a *really* fine brush.

Masking tape might seem like cheating, but for two things. First, you are an amateur and need all the help you can get. Second, even the pros use tape in certain situations.

When you buy any masking tape, be sure to buy brand name tape meant for work on automobiles and motorcycles. 3M sells some interesting products that make these jobs easier. For taping complex patterns with sharp curves, they make plastic tape. This material can be stretched into complex shapes without tearing like conventional masking tape. The other interesting material is called Fine Line Striping tape. The Fine Line tape is like having ten rolls of narrow tape combined on one cardboard tube. You roll the tape across the

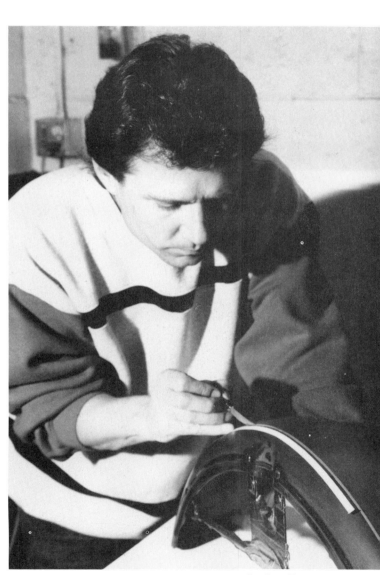

Brian puts the paint on a white card and takes the paint from that card and not the Dixie cup. This way, he is able to feel the consistency of the paint before applying it to the tank or fender. Mixing the paint to the correct thickness is a big part of learning to pinstripe.

Brian puts a straight line on the Sportster fender. Two different colors, magenta and dark pink, were used to create more impact than one color alone. Note the thin strip of masking tape used as a guide.

113

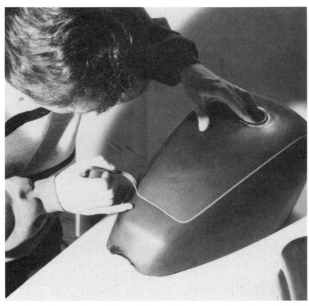

Brian starts on the tank with a very fine brush. He paints on the clear coat, which was scuffed with 600-grit sandpaper and will be covered with clear coat again after the pinstripes are finished.

tank, then pull out one of the pull outs. This leaves a thin stripe ready for paint with tape on either side of it. Need two lines? Just apply paint to the first pull out, then pull another and paint that one in a different color.

Gettin' Down to Business

What you need to get started is paint, a few brushes, some Prep Sol or a similar cleaner, and tape. A key part to laying down a nice clean line is learning to thin the paint correctly. Add too much thinner and the line spreads to either side and has no definition. Use too little thinner and the paint goes on too thick with dry spots where no paint made it from the brush to the tank.

Brian Truesdell, a pinstriper from St. Paul, Minnesota, mixes the paint in small, 3oz Dixie cups because they have no wax coating. Then he puts some of the paint on a white card and actually draws the paint from the card instead of the little cup. Using the card gives him a chance to pull the brush through the paint and feel just how thick it is before laying down a line.

Other painters just mix the paint in some kind of small cup and work from the cup. As a starting

The finished tank. Note the double stripe and the shine created by the clear coats sprayed on after the pinstriping was finished.

The next project is an elaborate pinstriping job by Lenny Schwartz at his shop in St. Paul, Minnesota. This paint job combines three techniques: pinstriping, airbrush, and gold leaf.

Lenny uses a variety of materials. On this job, most of the true pinstriping was done with urethane striping paint from House of Kolor. Short brushes with extremely long bristles are for pinstriping while the more conventional sign-painting brushes are used for lettering and special effects.

point, try one part paint to one-quarter part thinner. Mix it, see how it goes on, and then add thinner or paint to suit.

Before putting down a line, clean the surface thoroughly with Prep Sol or a similar solvent that leaves no residue. Once the surface is clean, you can apply the tape and begin the striping.

Pinstriping the Two-Tone
Candy Job from Chapter 7

Before the tank and fenders were taken to the striper, we wet-sanded the parts with 600-grit paper. The sanding gave us another opportunity to smooth and flatten the finish on the parts and the 600-grit scratches will give the striping paint something to bite into.

The parts were taken to B.T. Design in St. Paul. Brian Truesdell started by wiping down the parts with Windex glass cleaner to remove any oil left from handling the parts. He explained that because these parts were freshly painted and had not been handled too much, they did not need to be washed down with Prep Sol or a similar cleaner.

For the actual painting, Brian used One Shot enamel, mixed to the correct color in a 3oz Dixie cup.

The colors Brian chose are both violet, one a little darker than the other. We decided to use a simple design that would follow the color break with a double line. Brian put the darker shade over the darker part of our two-tone paint job. He applied most of the paint freehand, using masking tape as a guide along parts of the front fender. Pinstriping the Sportster took slightly more than one hour, then it was back to Mallard Teal's shop for the final coats of protective clear.

Cool Blue Stripes for
Fat Bob's Hot Flames

Jon Kosmoski does much of his own pinstriping, using the traditional pinstriping brushes and his own urethane striping enamel. For the flames painted on in Chapter 8, Jon chose light blue, a traditional color for outlining a set of flames.

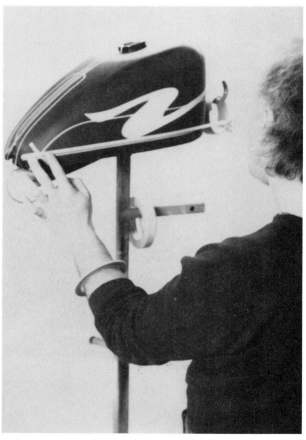

By laying on the tape in the correct sequence, Lenny will be able to pull the masking tape in sections. Once he starts, it will be a matter of pulling tape, painting, pulling tape, and painting again. By doing it in a specific sequence, the whole operation becomes much less time consuming.

The beginning of Lenny's design. The base paint is factory black, scuffed with a maroon Scotch-Brite pad. Before taping, Lenny wiped the tank down with Prep Sol.

116

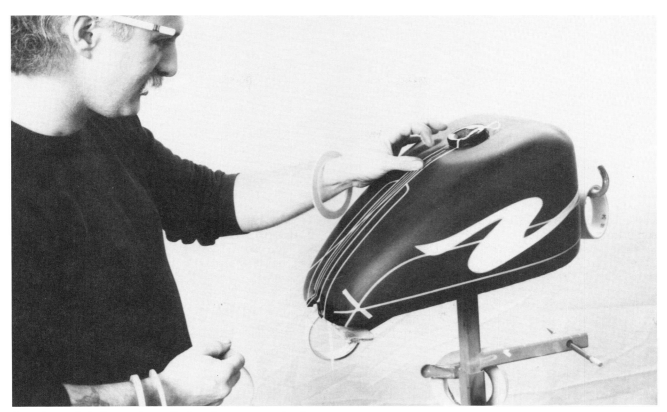

One-sixteenth-inch tape is applied to the center section by hand. These small strips of tape will create pinstripes in reverse when they are painted over and then removed.

The design on the center of the tank and the evolution of the taping on the sides of the tank. Paper is used to mask off the larger areas.

The tank just before the painting starts. The last step is to wipe the tank down with a tack rag before the spraying begins.

Lenny starts the painting with a touch-up gun running at 40psi. An air brush could have been used, too, though it takes longer. Lenny starts with a light, or bond, coat, followed by a heavier coat after the first coat has flashed over.

Jon started at the front of the tanks and worked back, drawing paint from a small piece of cardboard. He likes the ability to "feel" the thickness of the paint each time the brush is drawn through it on the card. For thinning the paint, Jon used a thinner designed specifically for the striping urethane. The urethane paint bites faster than the enamels, but there's still time to wipe off a mistake and start over.

Jon took his time with the job. "I don't do this as often as I should," he explained. "So it takes me longer than a guy who works at this every day. It is like everything else, if you want to be really good at striping you need to practice."

Jon's years of practice serve him well, and he soon moves on to the fenders. Because this is a single stripe, the job goes fast. Once the tanks are covered in a clear coat, Fat Bob's flames will be rimmed in blue and protected from UV rays and acid rain, too.

Two-Tone Stripes for Mallard's Wild Two-Tone Paint Job

Brian Truesdell, who pinstripes many of Mallard's paint jobs, has been striping for a number of

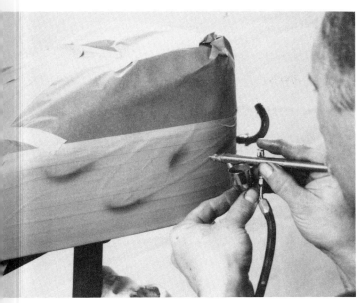

After painting in the sky blue on the center and the sides, those areas are taped over and violet shadows are sprayed on the side of the tank. Paint is urethane striping paint from House of Kolor. Paint is applied with a two-stage air brush which has a stepped trigger (trigger controls both air and material) like a full-sized gun. The material amount is controlled by how far back Lenny pulls the trigger.

Lenny sprays a dark violet on the band running along the bottom and the strip down the center of the tank after taping off the areas sprayed earlier.

years. When it came time to stripe the unique scallops on Mallard's bike, the hardest part was choosing the two colors.

Brian and Mallard worked for an hour, trying first one color and then another. Getting the right color often means mixing colors, and Brian was busy trying to come up with the two shades. Finally, the two painters agreed on a deep red and a bright teal but then could not decide which color to put inside and which to put outside the scallops.

Once the colors and their positions were determined, the rest was relatively easy. Brian started with the scallops on the tank (the parts had already been sprayed with clear coat and then scuffed with 600-grit paper) and moved on to the other pieces. As always, the last step was another three coats of clear coat to give the parts a great shine and to protect the fine line-work.

Lenny Schwartz Does More than Just a Simple Set of Pinstripes

Pinstripes are normally thought of as an accent to the larger paint job. Lenny Schwartz of Krazy Kolors in St. Paul, Minnesota, sometimes does pinstripe and airbrush work that becomes so elaborate that it becomes the paint job rather than an accent to the paint job.

The paint job seen here started out with a Sportster tank and fenders painted factory black. Lenny began by scuffing the black paint with a

maroon Scotch-Brite pad. Like using very fine sandpaper, this treatment will give the pinstriping paint a good surface to grab onto.

Lenny likes to draw out his designs on paper before starting in with the long skinny brushes. He decided to combine pinstriping with gold leaf and air brush work. For the area to be covered in gold leaf, he cut out the shape and taped it to the tank to double check the design. The flowing shape seemed right, so he traced the outline of the pattern on the tank with a stabilla pencil. Available in art supply houses, the stabilla pencil marks can be painted right over—in fact, Lenny says you have to paint over the marks or they show up after the painting is finished.

Over the years, Lenny has learned to tape off a design like this one so he can paint in stages, untaping the parts as he goes. It requires thinking and taping in reverse. The areas that get painted last should be masked off first. "Once I learned how to tape," he explained, "I could do elaborate designs in one day that used to take me three or four."

After taping off the design on the tank, Lenny started the spraying with a small touch-up gun, running at 40psi. He started with a light coat (what some call a bond coat). He waited for that to flash over and then put on a heavier coat on the center and along the bottom of the gas tank. Next, he got out the air brush (running at 20psi) and added dark areas or shadows under the flowing pattern that will later be done in gold leaf. Lenny often uses shadows and highlights to create a 3-D effect, and give depth to his designs.

119

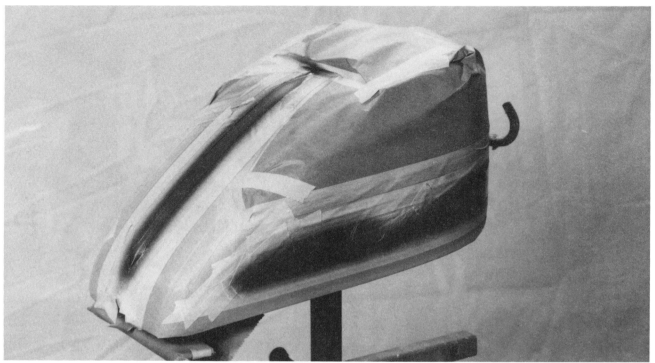

*The tank after areas in the center and along the bottom
of the tank have been sprayed in violet.*

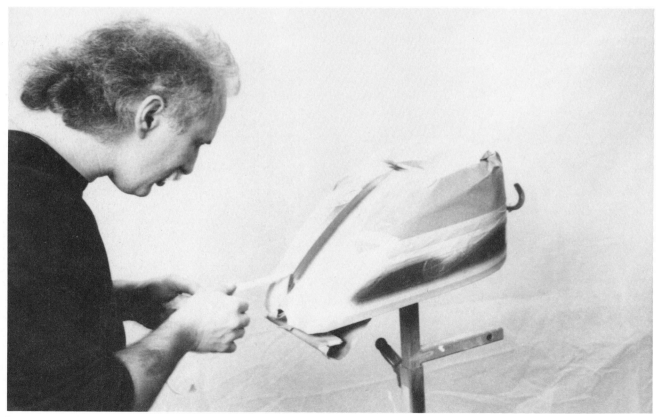

Lenny starts to pull the tape off the tank.

120

Lenny pulls the thin tape on the center of the tank. By spraying over this tape, he created a pinstripe in reverse.

After adding the shadows, Lenny taped over the areas already air brushed and uncovered the center of the tank and a strip along the bottom of the tank. The first area was sprayed light blue, the new area was sprayed violet. Pasted to the center section of the gas tank was a design laid out with ultra-thin masking tape. When the thin tape was pulled off, there was a series of thin black lines—pinstripes in reverse—and another example of the planning that went into this job (if this sounds confusing, check the photos).

The next job was the gold leaf on the sides of the tank. Lenny first applied the sizing or heavy adhesive that the actual gold leaf would stick to, using the outline traced onto the tank earlier with the stabilla pencil. The sizing must dry to a tacky condition. "Wait until it is wet enough to just put a fingerprint on when you touch it," Lenny advised, "but not so wet that it strings up onto your finger."

The gold leaf comes in sheets and is available in a variety of styles. This job called for variegated leaf and Lenny started by sticking one sheet onto the sizing near the front of the tank. The variegated gold leaf has a pattern running through it. The next sheet of leaf must be matched up with the first so the pattern continues without any apparent seams. Lenny uses a small, soft brush to push the gold leaf into good contact with the sizing and

Now it is easy to see why the center and sides have to be taped and untaped separately. Note the thin reversed pinstripes in this close-up. The tank will pick up a great shine when the final clear coats are applied.

121

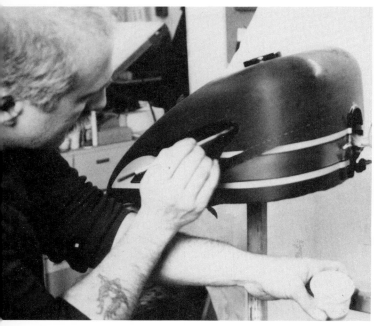

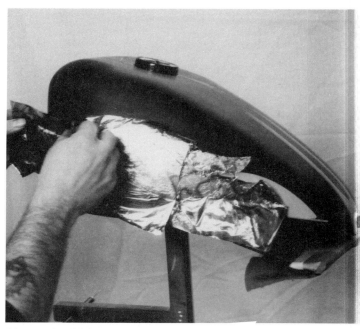

Lenny brushes on the sizing (think of it as adhesive) to which the gold leaf will stick. Again, note the outline marked out earlier with a stabilla pencil. Sizing should be just tacky when the leaf is applied.

Sheets of gold leaf are not big enough to stretch across the tank. Shown is a patterned, variegated leaf. Patterns must be matched up where the sheets meet, much the way you would match up sheets of wallpaper.

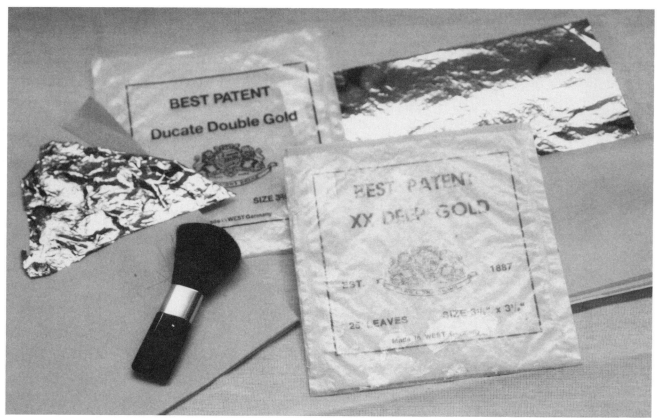

Gold leaf comes in thin sheets available at art supply and sign supply stores. The sheets of gold are very thin and must be handled with care. Gold leaf is usually applied with a soft brush.

work out the inevitable bubbles. Once the leaf is stuck to the sizing, it should sit overnight. The next task is to gently tear away the extra gold leaf, which is not stuck to the sizing, with that same little brush. Areas near the edge that will not tear off can be pulled free with a little masking tape.

Lenny did not think that the tanks were finished, yet. After the gold leaf was completely dry, he pinstriped the design in the center of the tank. While he was at it, a few more lines done freehand seemed like a good idea. These freehand lines are reminiscent of work done by Von Dutch with very fine lines intersecting and spreading into a design of their own. Next, Lenny pinstriped the edges of the gold leaf, being careful to paint over the outline left earlier by the stabilla pencil.

The final touch in this rather elaborate design (or series of designs) is the splash of paint added to the center and along the sides in magenta. To do this work, Lenny chose a sign-painting brush with short bristles and brushed on a design that looked good to his eye. To give this new magenta splash more definition, Lenny highlighted the top of the design and created shadows on the bottom.

In the end, Lenny had created a unique paint job. Part air brush, part gold leaf, and part pin-stripe, it shows what can be done with skill, patience, and imagination.

Your First Pinstripe Job

If you are ready to try a little pinstriping, consider using fine line tape to create a simple design. Follow the basics, learn to thin the paint correctly and do not be afraid to give it a try—you can always wipe off your mistakes and start over. The project seen here shows how Lenny Schwartz created a set of four stripes across a Fat Bob tank.

Like any striping operation, the parts must be clean, and you have to be sure the tape is stuck well to the metal so the paint cannot migrate under its edges. The tape comes in two versions, with different numbers of pull outs. After putting on the tape, it is just a matter of pulling one or more pull outs, painting and then pulling the tape. The only real problem to using this tape is the fact that it does not bend, so you either have to limit your design or learn to do a little freehand work in the curves.

Give It a Try

If you have never considered doing your own pinstriping, you now have just enough information

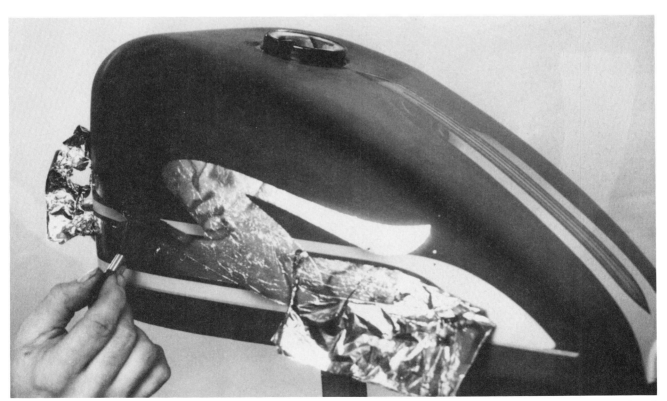

Gold leaf is so fragile that the areas not stuck to the sizing are just brushed away with a soft brush (this is a makeup brush but any soft brush would do). The brush is also used to carefully brush out any air bubbles. Leaf should be left on the sizing overnight before you brush away the edges. Gold leaf is available in different styles, including silver leaf.

Here we see the right side with the gold leaf in place. Masking tape can be used to pull off gold leaf at edges that will not break off with the soft brush.

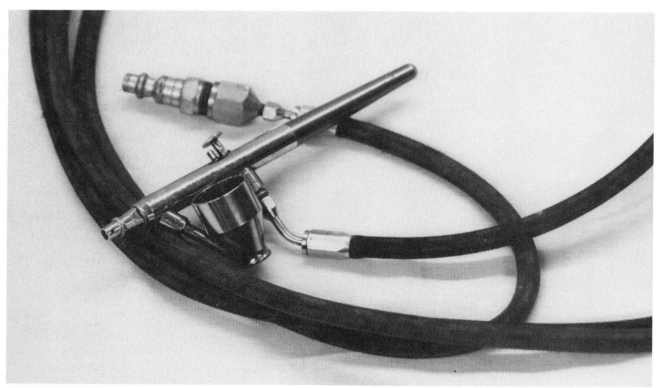

Lenny's air brush with two-stage trigger. Think of it as a small paint gun that runs at 20psi.

to be dangerous. Trot down to the local paint supply store, buy some paint, tape, and thinner and give it a try. If it does not work out, wipe it off. If it looks great, you will have the satisfaction of knowing that you did it yourself.

After all the masking tape is removed, it is time to pinstripe the sky blue area on the center of the tank. Note that Lenny rests his other hand on the gas cap filler, not on the paint where the oils from his hand could collect.

A well-worn veteran, this little touch-up gun is a good fit when an air brush is too small and a full-sized gun is too big.

Some fine freehand work. Note the Dixie cup and how one hand is used to support and steady the other.

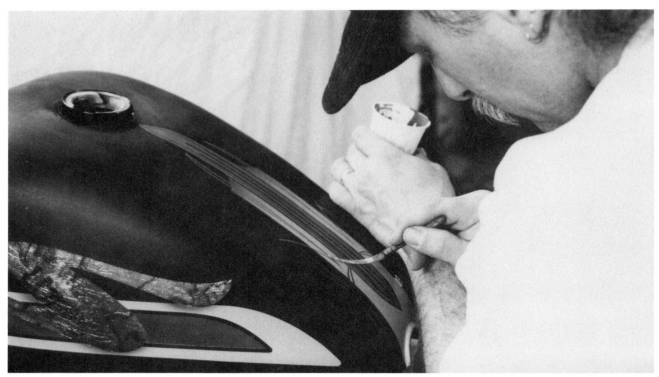

Lenny continues the design with more thin, VonDutch-style pinstripes.

After year's of practice Lenny has learned to control the brush to the extent necessary to produce some nice free-hand work.

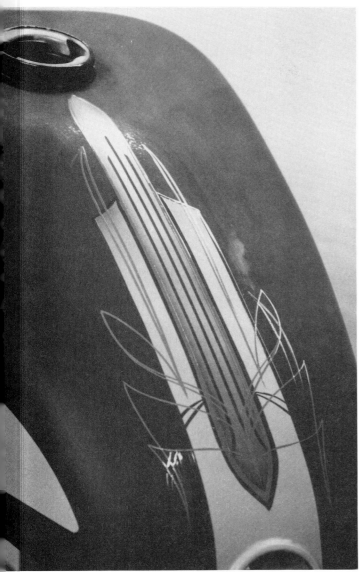

The center of the tank after Lenny is finished with the freehand pinstripes.

Feeling that the tank needs something more, Lenny adds a freehand design with a sign-painting brush.

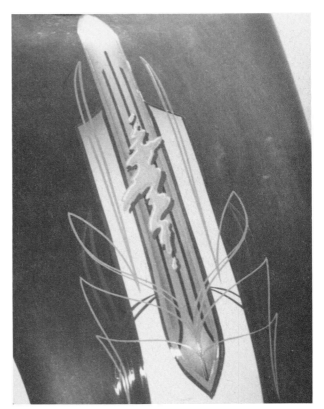

The center of the tank. Note that the design has been outlined and shadowed so that it seems to pop out of the tank.

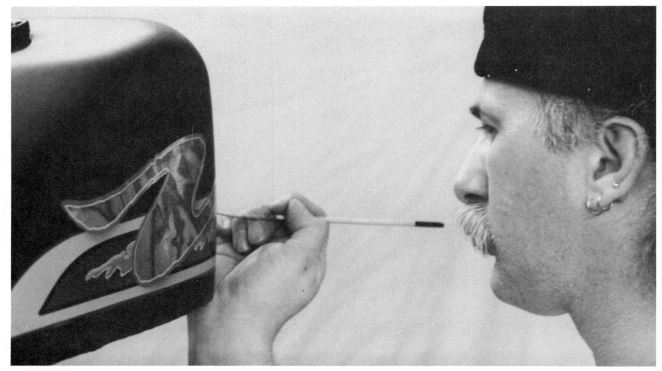

Lenny adds a similar design to the sides of the tank, using outlines and shadows again to give the design a 3-D effect.

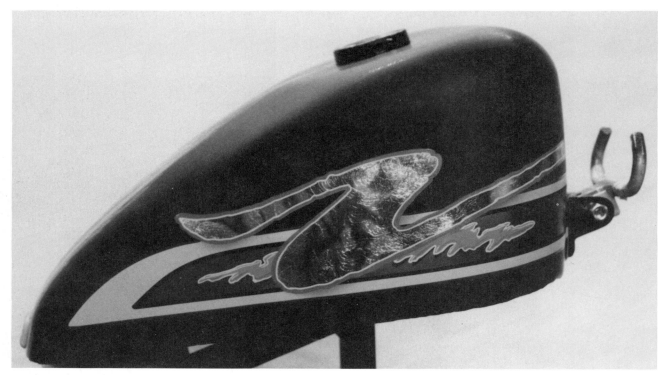

Close-up of the finished tank sides shows the gold leaf with pinstripes and the carefully outlined design near the bottom of the tank.

Jon Kosmoski starts on the Fat Bob tanks seen in Chapter 8. Note how his little finger steadies his hand.

Even though Jon starts the job with clean hands, he tries not to touch the tanks any more than necessary.

Learning to paint a neat, clean curve takes practice. You do not want to stop in the middle of a curve.

The finished tank. Curves are smooth and graceful. Striping cleans up the edge where the flames meet the tank and makes the flames stand out clearly.

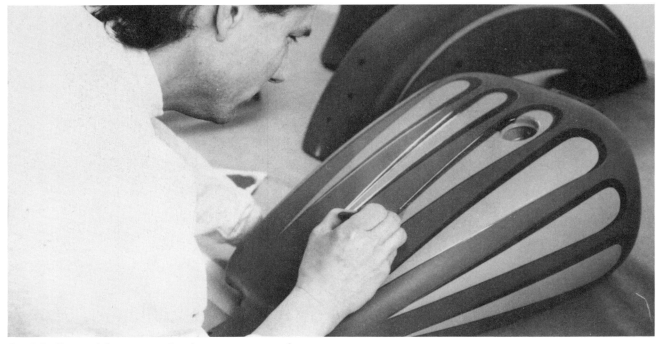

Straight lines might seem easier than curves; yet a long straight pull is one of the toughest techniques to master.

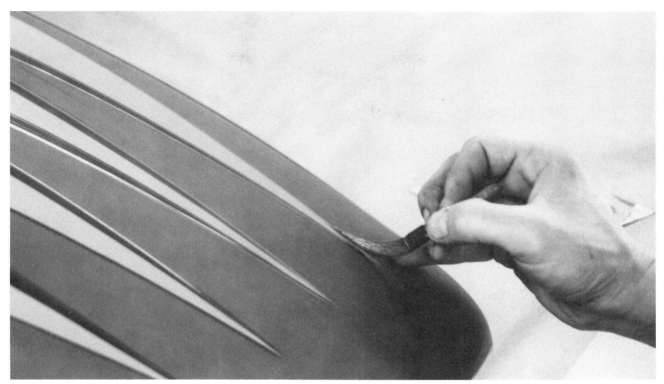

The long, skinny brush holds much paint, making it possible to run a long line without continually dipping the brush in paint. Note the little finger supporting the hand.

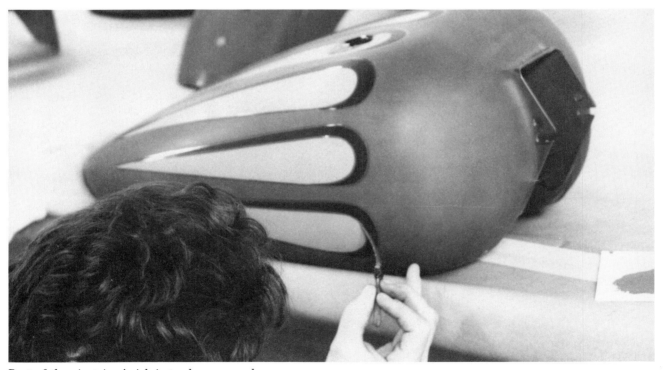

Part of the pinstriper's job is to clean up and cover any rough edges so that seams like this one have a nice even curve.

The finished product, though it still needs to be covered with clear coat. Choosing colors for a job like this is tough, as the pinstripe colors need to contrast with the two main colors on the tank without clashing too severely.

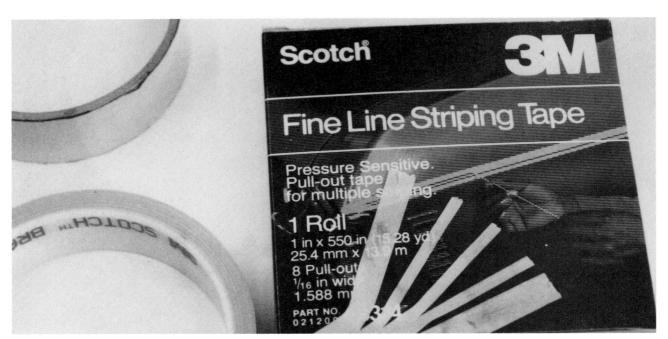

Painters use this 3M Fine Line tape to do some easy pinstriping. The tape comes in two versions, each with a different number of pull outs.

Apply the Fine Line tape straight across the tank, making sure it is stuck tightly to the surface.

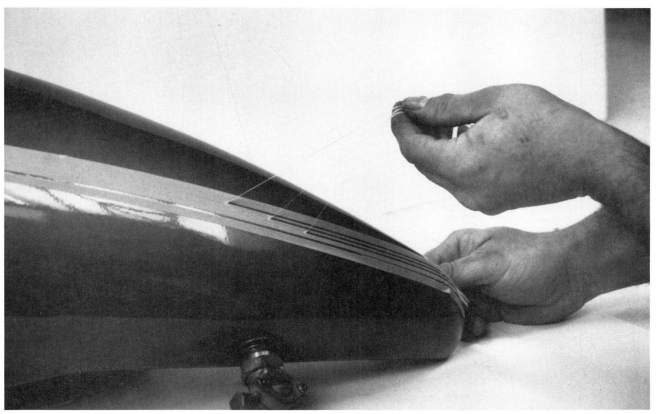

Next, remove as many pull outs as you deem necessary.

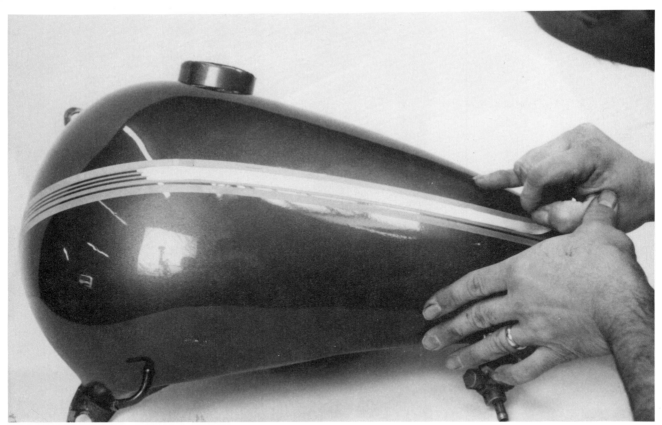

Then, lay on the paint. Different colors can be used, of course, for a more dramatic effect.

When you have finished painting, pull the tape and you have a great pinstriping job. Lie to your friends and tell 'em you did it free hand.

Sources

Eric Aurand
480 North Front Street
North Libery, IA 52317-0264
designer/illustrator

Crazy Colors
Lenny Schwartz
453 West 7th Street
St. Paul, MN 55102
paint striping

B.T. Design
Brian Truesdell
937 Smith Avenue
St. Paul, MN 55118
pinstriping

Mallard Teal
Payne Avenue Auto Body
860 Payne Avenue
St. Paul, MN 55101
custom paint work

Mattson Spray Equipment
230 West Coleman
Rice Lake, WI 54868
HVLP paint equipment

House of Kolor
Jon Kosmoski
2521 27th Avenue South
Minneapolis, MN 55406
custom paint supplies

Graco/Croix Air
Customer Service
1-800-328-0211
Tim Whelan
(612) 623-6615
HVLP paint equipment

Binks
Bill Mott
Griggs Midway Building
1821 University
St. Paul, MN
spray painting equipment

Strip Rite
7901 Beech Street Northeast
Fridley, MN 55432
paint stripping

Index